Peter F. Drucker was named 'The Father of Modern Management' because he changed forever the way we look at management.

What he did was to place it into the centre of our ever changing society.

What he believed was that management is based upon ethical responsibility and should improve the lives of everyone.

He is recognised as one of the outstanding contributor of the 20th century whose influence is still ongoing.

# PETER F. DRUCKER

## The Landmarks of his Ideas

**Peter Starbuck**

lulu.com

**Peter F. Drucker: The Landmarks of his Ideas**

Published by Peter Starbuck

Copyright Dr Peter Starbuck 2012

Peter Starbuck asserts the moral right to be identified as the author of this work

ISBN No: 978-1-4710-1053-8

Printed by lulu.com

*With Thanks to the Team*

*Sue Edwards, Rob Jackson, Brian Jones, Mike Robinson*

*and my wife Heather Starbuck*

*Also to Jac Jones for his illustration*

# CONTENTS

| | |
|---|---|
| Introduction | 9 |
| Drucker's schooldays in Vienna (1909-1925) | 11 |
| His early adulthood in Hamburg, Germany and the discovery of his 'ethics as the foundation for his 'society' (1925-1927) | 15 |
| His transfer to Frankfurt and the foundations for a 'workable society' (1927-1933) | 22 |
| His arrival in England (1933-1937) | 26 |
| His chance meeting with his wife-to-be | 29 |
| The move to American and his 'economic foundation' (1937) | 34 |
| His life in America | 40 |
| His break into management | 47 |
| His answer to management – (MbO) | 56 |
| His next batch of ideas | 65 |
| His own seventieth birthday present | 83 |
| His last major venture at eighty-one-years of age | 89 |
| Drucker at ninety-years-of-age | 102 |
| Overview | 117 |
| About the Author | 122 |
| Bibliography | 125 |
| Index | 133 |

# Introduction

More than six years have passed since Peter Drucker died. Normally when someone who has recognition of being prominent in their field dies, their passing is marked by a few obituaries and tributes and maybe a biography of their work. This is the conclusion as their memory fades away. In exceptionally rare cases of one in several million people something different happens. Peter Drucker is a case in point. The exceptional happening is that interest in their work from a high activity base increases beyond any anticipation.

The evidence in Drucker's case is that in the English language prior to his death there had been six biographical books written about his work over a fifteen year period. In contrast, double that number have been published since his death.

Also Drucker Societies are established in every continent around the world. At the last count they numbered eighty with a significant cluster in China.

Drucker is now being more written about, studied, and practised than at any other time since his ideas emerged in the mid-1930s. This is surprising when you consider his distinguished multi-faceted career as a journalist, intellectual, lawyer, banker, lecturer, consultant and art expert. In many of these activities he had received international recognition.

What this is proving is that Drucker's idea are timeless, and most are at least as relevant today as when they were first recorded. It has been assessed that Drucker's writing in his forty-plus books and other written works amounts to at least ten million words equalling twelve Bibles or eleven Complete Works of Shakespeare. Few people have time to read a fraction of Drucker's messages. This book is a guide to give an overview of the management thinker who has out-written everyone else in his field, and is the most written about, because what he had to say was relevant in his day and is still relevant, not only for today but also for the future.

Why Drucker believed that management was so essential was that it is the collection of the activities in our lives that affects everything we do. Properly understood and applied it has the capability of changing our own lives for the better, forever.

Peter Starbuck

Oswestry, Shropshire, UK

January 2012

## Drucker's schooldays in Vienna (1909-1925)

Peter F. Drucker was born on 19 November 1909 in Vienna, and died in Claremont, California on 11 November 2005. As he progressed into old age he wrote that he had lived through all of the major events of the twentieth-century, which he had.

The Viennese records show that his parents were Jewish by birth, but converted to Lutheran Christianity before his birth. They were married in a civil ceremony rather than in a Synagogue, which indicates that they were non-conforming Jews. Drucker's father (Dr Jur) Adolf Bertram Drucker was born on 27 August 1875 in Izkany Bukowina, which was part of the Austrian/Hungarian Empire that has subsequently been divided between Romania and the Ukraine. He died in America in 1967. Adolf's parents were Heinrich Drucker and Marie (nee Schönfeld). His mother Karoline Drucker was born on 29 July 1885 in Vienna in the 9th District of Wiederhofgasse 7, daughter of Ferdinand Bondi (Bondy) and Bertha Bondi (nee Berger). Both Drucker and his younger brother Gerhard Augustin, born 23 August 1911, were christened shortly after their birth, Drucker on 24 December 1909.

His birth certificate says that he was born into a Protestant Community. His place of birth was Vienna, 19th District, Döblinger,

Haupstrasse No 42. What is recorded is that in April 1909 his parents were living in the 2nd District of Untere Augartenstrasse 40, which was the Jewish area. Their address was Haidgasse No 7. There exists a HEIMATSCHEIN for his father, which is a certificate of authority for a Jew to be entitled to live at his home in his own country of Austria. Haidgasse was a prosperous area of four to five storey apartments. Döblinger was an affluent location with individually-designed substantial homes.

Drucker's father was a principal civil servant. His mother he describes as having attended lectures by Sigmund Freud. There is no conspicuous record that she continued her medical interest beyond this point.

He described that his mother arranged dinners at their home for members of the Viennese intelligentsia, which included leading politicians, writers, artists and economists in a Vienna that was one of the intellectual centres of the world. The continuity of these events in Drucker's young life was severely disrupted by the turmoil in the Austrian/Hungarian Empire. This began on 28 June 1914 when the heir to the Austrian throne, Archduke Franz Ferdinand, and his wife were assassinated by the Serbian, Gavrilo Princip. The Austrians reacted by invading Serbia, thus precipitating World War I. He describes the situation as being *'torn by explosive internal discontent and bitter strife between a dozen discordant "nationalists"'*.

By the end of the conflict, Austria was defeated, had lost its Empire and was bankrupt, with inflation reported at such multiples that prices by 1922 had risen seventy-five thousand times compared with 1914, as the currency became almost worthless.

As the soldiers returned from the war following defeat, they found that they had lost almost everything at home. Consequently Drucker remarked that *'everybody was poor'*, as the population of Vienna were on subsistence rations, while the children were prevented from death by starvation only through the programmes of the victorious allies' relief organisations.

Social tensions were exacerbated by the political extremes of the left and right. As a result of their challenge the Emperor was forced to abdicate on 11 November 1918 as a Socialist-dominated republic was declared. Consequently the socialists failed to halt government spending, resulting in the economy spiralling out of control. When the financial crisis peaked in 1922, austerity measures of reducing welfare expenditure were imposed, even at the risk of causing high unemployment.

This action created relative stability, though at an impoverished level. All of this turmoil was having an effect on the growing Drucker who, when taking part in a Republican Day commemoration rally on 11 November 1923, made a self-discovery that he was *a bystander*, as he discarded his banner and returned home. He said that the fact that he was a bystander was only a discovery because bystanders were born and not made. He later wrote that bystanders have enjoyment but they never achieve what the self-dedicated megalomaniacs achieve by concentrating on their sole objectives.

While all this upheaval was taking place Drucker progressed through his primary schooling. For the first three years he received standard schooling. At the age of nine he moved to the fourth grade of progressive junior school, which he records as one of the most significant periods of his intellectual development. His teachers were Miss Elsa and Miss Sophy Reiss, whom he credits with shaping his life by teaching him how to learn, and self-develop by emphasising his strengths and aptitudes, eliminating his weaknesses and then analysing his progress. This would be the basis for his managerial idea of organisation: identifying their unique excellence as their strategic aim. It was later termed "core competence". This school was the domain of the Reiss sisters and housed in premises owned by Dr Eugenia Schwarzwald (1872-1940), who is still celebrated in Vienna as an education pioneer. After completing the fourth grade at his junior school as a ten-year-old, he gained entry to the Vienna Gymnasium a year earlier than standard. His attendance at the Gymnasium he described as 'not stimulating' as he found learning Greek and Latin grammar boring although he found the works of the Greek philosophers appealing and he quoted them throughout his working career. He credits his adolescent development to attending 'salons', some of which were arranged by Dr Schwarzwald. At the salons he had to present to, and then argue his ideas with, adults. Despite the austerity, *salons* were an integrated part of Viennese intellectual life, reflecting that it still remained one of the outstanding intellectual centres of the period, with its World league composers, authors, artists, philosophers, and economists, some of whom were natives of the city while others were attracted émigrés.

**His early adulthood in Hamburg, Germany and the discovery of his 'ethics' as the foundation for his 'society' (1925-1927).**

As a seventeen year old plus, Drucker finished school, and asked his father to find him something in business, although his father's ambition was for him to go to university. His father's search found him a job as an apprentice clerk in an ironmongery export business in Hamburg. His time in Hamburg was a watershed in his intellectual development as he enrolled at Hamburg University as a doctoral student in the law faculty, while in full-time employment.

He recalled, as a non-German national, he was not permitted to practise general law, but was eligible to enrol for international law. As the regime allowed students to attend lectures or otherwise, this left him with a considerable amount of free time; this free time he described as spending five weekday evenings in the library where *'for fifteen months I read, and read, and read in German, English and French'*.

This time in Hamburg also marked the beginning of the acceleration of his intellectual development that would result in him being amongst the most eclectic writers on management and its related topics. That his education concentrated on the Germanic Gestalt holistic thought philosophy is apparent in his work, as it enabled him to see connections between activities and events that would not only change the value of the sum of the individual parts, but could change their outcomes. In understanding Drucker, it has to be appreciated that his holistic analysis and synthesis is so ingrained in him that it is part of his persona.

As a student's concession he was allowed one free visit to the Hamburg Opera each week. He tells us that the most consequential and lasting impression of the performance came from Giuseppe Fortunio Francesco Verdi (1813-1901), who wrote his most demanding work 'Falstaff', at the age of eighty. He said that Verdi's life aim and achievement left a lasting impression on him; Drucker promised himself, as Verdi did, that he would work all of his life continually learning, and striving to make his next work the best.

It is the development of Drucker's thought processes, and the commitment to Verdi's policy of *continual self-development*, that goes a long way to explaining the manner of how he worked, which made it possible for him to make his unique contribution. Because of his eclectic research into every topic that interested him, the outcome could have been that his work was complex, defused and confused. Fortunately the outcome was quite the contrary, as one of his hallmarks of his work is his ability to express himself in the clearest of terms. This is an admirable achievement in itself, but even more so when it is realised that he was not writing in his mother tongue.

To describe the times in Europe of his development as 'disturbed' is an understatement. More appropriately the political situation is better described as a cauldron of events. Karl Heinrich Marx (1818-1883) was in the ascendancy and communism had been established in Russia. The Germany Weimar government was incompetent, and would be overthrown by Adolf Hitler's (1889-1945) totalitarian Nazism, which was preceded by Benito Mussolini's (1883-1945) fascism in Italy. Everywhere one looked in Europe, strikes and civil unrest, or revolution, were the order of the day.

His personal reaction was to embark on an intellectual journey to attempt to make sense out of life. This was a four-part journey which began with an attempt to discover a *purpose for living*: this is the foundation for his Ethics.

The answer to his set question he discovered in the work of the depressive religious reactionary Danish Protestant Søren Aabye Kierkegaard (1813-1855) through his book 'Fear and Trembling' (1843). Drucker wrote that this book had such an immediate impact on him that he found '*HIM.*' He continued that he needed to have an existential dimension to his life, and advised his audience that a belief should be part of their life balance. Why Kierkegaard is such an important influence on him is confirmed in his several times published essay 'The Unfashionable Kierkegaard' (Autumn 1949).

What he explains is that Kierkegaard retells that God commanded Abraham to make the ultimate sacrifice and take his favourite son Isaac to the mountain of Moviah, and kill him. Against all his instincts Abraham obeys God's command. As he is about to plunge the knife into Isaac, God relents, and Isaac is spared. For Drucker the messages from Kierkegaard are that, we must learn to hate before we can learn to love, and that we must learn to die before we can learn to live.

Although Drucker's theological journey to discover his *purpose for living* is extensive, and includes amongst his influences Thomas Aquinas (1223-1274), Martin Luther (1483-1546), Jean Calvin (1509-1564), and Max Weber (1864-1920), it is the impact of the Russian Fyodor Michaelovitch Dostoevsky (1821-1881) through his book 'The Grand Inquisitor' (1880) that completes the answer to Drucker's quest.

For Drucker, Dostoevsky's basic message is that in life there occur some very difficult decisions, which most of us would prefer to avoid making. The Grand Inquisitor has the answer, and proposes that if you surrender yourselves to him he will relieve you of the problems, and make the decisions for you. Also as he is making the decisions they are all his responsibility. If the decisions are sinful as he is making them, it is him who is sinning and not you. Drucker's conclusion is that this acceptance of the Grand Inquisitor's offer is an abdication of a basic Christian principle: no matter how difficult personal decisions are throughout our lives, we are committed to make them, and accept them, and take personal responsibility.

Consequently, Drucker was amongst those who not only recognised Dostoevsky's warning of the danger of abdicating Christian responsibility, but also that Dostoevsky's proposition was a harbinger of the prospect of the Grand Inquisitor emerging, which he did in the form of Hitler. With the conjoining of Kierkegaard's and Dostoevsky's fundamental ideas, the foundation of the first part of Drucker's intellectual journey – his ethical *purpose for living* – was in place. The importance of this discovery is that it is the foundation of his management idea, which must start and finish with ethical behaviour, integrity, and responsibility. This basically is the foundation for his Ethics.

For him, ethics are not an option for the manager — they are the core of the profession of management. It is the basis for every decision. He encapsulated the position when he summarises that managers come from every walk of life, from every society, and that they had human strengths, and weaknesses, as all human beings. Providing it did not impair their job performance these were acceptable. In contrast, what was never acceptable, were managers who lacked *integrity*, because they were a corrupting influence on those they managed. Anyone in this category must be banned as a manager. This was the practical basis for Drucker's business ethics. As a general view, Drucker believed that managers were better people if they had a 'faith' and could see merit in Confucianism's respect for other people, although his own 'faith' was Christianity. One of his last reflections was recorded in an interview with James Nelson.

Nelson: 'Now you're 95, what about the after-life, what about God? How are you thinking about the moment of transition that you are approaching?

Drucker: I happen to be very a conventional, very traditional Christian, Period. I don't think about it, I'm told it's not my job to think about it. My job is to say, yes Sir.

Nelson: This must be very comforting?

Drucker:    It is.  And every morning and evening I say praise be to God for the beauty of His creation.  Amen'. (Nelson circa 2004/05)

Having found the *purpose for living* as the next part of his intellectual journey Drucker needed to discover a society in which its citizens could live in <u>freedom</u> and with a <u>purpose</u>.  What he envisaged was not a utopian, but a *workable society*.  With his objective, open-minded approach he examined the alternatives and concluded that Marx's communism lacked a social system, and also was flawed economically.  His reasoning for concluding that it was not a social system was because it failed at the first hurdle of his ethical society, which was based upon Christian Protestantism that recognised that all humans were uniquely individualistic, whose preferences, providing they were legal, society had to accommodate.  Drucker's conclusion of Marx was that individual freedom had to be sacrificed in the interest of the collective masses.  Consequently there was no capacity for individual purpose in a collective society.

Hitler's Nazi totalitarianism Drucker also considered as a *workable society* but rejected it at the first hurdle by failing to prove the ethical purpose of the combination of Kierkegaard and Dostoevsky's tests.  Also as with Marx's communism, it was collectively anti-individual, and failed to provide a purpose for living, as the only recognition was death.

## His transfer to Frankfurt and his foundations for a 'workable society' (1927-1933)

After fifteen months in Hamburg Drucker transferred his studies to Frankfurt University and also began work for an old merchant bank that had been taken over by a Wall Street brokerage business. A publication in September 1929 by him, on why the New York stock market would continue to prosper he admitted was fatally flawed, as two days later the Wall Street crash occurred. He recounted that nothing remains of the publication as it *'disappeared without trace a few days later so did my job'* (Drucker 2002: ix). He wrote that after this salutary lesson he vowed never to make financial forecasts again.

He eventually joined the editorial staff as an economics, and current affairs editor for the 'Frankfurter General Anzeiger', which is still regarded as an *institution*. While at the paper he travelled throughout the near East and Europe, where he attended, amongst other major events, the Geneva Disarmament Conference and the League of Nations. This event signalled that he had embarked on a life-time career as a writer.

Although he eventually became recognised as a polymath it was his writing that was one of the cores of his life as confirmed during an interview: when he was asked what he did, he replied '*I write*'.

After four years of study in 1931 he submitted his thesis 'Die Rechtfertigung des Volkerrechts aus dem Staatswillen' (The Justification of International Law and the Will of the State) published in 1933. The thesis examined the two theories of international law that had developed post-World War I in the hope that they would facilitate world peace. The two recognised theories were the 'theory of self-imposed obligation' and the 'theory of agreement'. His thesis compares and argues the case vigorously for both constructively, and comes to the conclusion that, as with Catholic Natural Law it is only the 'theory of agreement' that should prevail; this is because it is the only treatise that anchors the law that established a satisfactory basis for international law, and established an absolute system of values. The outcome was that he was awarded his Doctorate of Law (Dr Jur), which mirrored his father's qualification. He now added a further credential to that of being a writer — that of an academic, which he always disclaimed, as he regarded himself as an intellectual.

After the completion of his doctorate he carried out some part-time lecturing at Frankfurt and was invited to become a 'Dozent' or registered lecturer, which in Germany was a step towards becoming a professor. It was a position that he never formalised.

Having researched his ideas on international law as a foundation for world-wide social justice he returned to his ongoing objective – to find a *workable society*. By 26 April 1933 JCB Mohr, who were described as Germany's most famous publishers, produced as No 100 in a series of monographs, Drucker's thirty-two page 'Fr J Stahl; Konservative Staatslehre & Geschichtliche Entwicklung Motrtueringan' (Fr J Stahl; Conservative Theory of the State and Historical Development). Frederich Julius Stahl (1802-1861), a Christian converted Jew was a German politician and university academic who proposed a conservative society. The basis of his argument was for an equitable society that was monarchical Christian-founded. The monarchical head of the country would uphold the constitution, and protect democratic government. In return the citizens would support the monarch, and act in their mutual self-interest. Stahl's political philosophy was described as 'throne and altar'.

Drucker's monograph on Stahl is still regarded as the *'locus classicus'* of someone who is described as a most difficult-to-understand conservative figure in German politics.

Drucker stated that he wrote this work to make it clear that he opposed the ideas of the Nazis, as he contentiously promoted a democratic alternative ideology by a Jew. After the publication, having made his point, he prudently left for his native Austria. The following month, 'book burning took place in every German university town. The books were by Jews who were traitors and renegades'. (Elon 2002: 395).

Although he never visited the USA, Stahl had strong reason to believe that it may have had the best working society. This was a view that Drucker shared, from the influence of Alexis de Tocqueville (1805-1859), who had had two prolonged visits to America which enabled him to gather material for his two volumes 'Democracy in America' (1835 & 1840). He described the population as being interested in government, free to promote their ideas, obsessed with change, and self-interest. He also recorded that the population was dedicated to making money. Drucker did not mention de Tocqueville's recall of their money-making attitudes, but was attracted by the freedom of expression, and their pluralistic attitude towards society. His search for the components for a working society was extensive as he considered the English parliamentarians of Edmund Burke's (1729-1797) era while rejecting the French Revolutionaries. He later examined the work of the American Founding Fathers and its impact on Federalism and Pluralism, which was all part of a continue review of the changes in society in general and in America in particular.

After a short stay in Austria, Drucker left for England, and later recorded that since his early teens he had wanted to leave Austria '*to leave the old behind*'. With him he took the first two parts of his intellectual journey of discovery, his ethical *purpose for living*, and a belief that the USA could provide a *workable society*.

## His arrival in England (1933-1937)

Arriving in England in the summer of 1933 he first worked as an insurance analyst. After returning from his parent's home in Vienna in the New Year of 1934 his new employment was with a London-based merchant bank as an assistant to the senior partner before progressing to become an analyst, economist, and eventually a banker. This marked a further career development. However, although it was a career that lasted for only three of the four years that he was in England, it was still an important part of his development for his later career.

Regarding his other careers, his lecturing was put on hold while his writing continued. In 1936, a paper was published in Austria by Gsur u Co Wein 'Die Judenfrage in Deutschland' (The Jewish Question in Germany). The pamphlet is dedicated to his father *'with love and admiration'* and is described as being mainly finished in 1933. The pamphlet summarises that the Jewish people are a tribe without a state, many of whom although belonging to a country, do not fully integrate. Comparing the major European countries of Britain, France and Germany, he concludes that they have been more integrated in

Germany, and that many more were proportionally successful than in the other two countries. The Nazis were now separating them and driving them into ghettos and emphasising their identity by giving them Jewish names. Drucker tells the Jews that they have a choice. If they choose to be Jewish it *'would merely be water of the mills of the Nazis so now of all times Jews have to be German and insist on their Germaness'*.

What he is demonstrating is that as a member of a *workable society* one has to have a social conscience for other threatened members.

Evidence exists of other writings that he did while in England. The work is another landmark in his career as a writer, being his first published work in English, in a book. It is 'GERMANY The Last Four Years: An Independent Examination of the Results of National Socialism' by *Germanicus* (1937), who were a collaboration of writers including Drucker.

It is a reproduction of major features that had appeared in 'The Banker' (the Organ of British Banking February 1937) together with some later articles under the title of 'Germany: The Results of 4 Years of National Socialism' by *Germanicus*. It is the work of about a dozen men of some achievement in Germany's military, financial and industrial affairs. To maintain their anonymity the authors are *Germanicus*. What the book does is dispute German official statistical reports on the economy, balance of trade and banking. It reports that the food of the population had been cut to bring it in line with the subsistence rationing that has been proved that combat soldiers could survive on. The only statistic that was not readily disputed was the Autobahn road-building programme. Within a fortnight of the book being published, it was banned in Germany. Regardless 'The Banker' continued to publish similar features on the Germany economy into 1940. When the Library of Congress in Washington DC attributed Drucker as '*Germanicus*', he had the details corrected to record that he was only a contributor.

Among the other important events which occurred while he was resident in London, was that he attended the lectures of John Maynard Keynes (1883-1947) at Cambridge University during the period when Keynes was completing his 'The General Theory of Employment, Interest, and Money' (1936). Drucker claimed to be the only person to have heard the lectures of the two greatest economists of the twentieth-century, Keynes and Schumpeter, as he recalled that he attended Joseph Schumpeter's (1883-1950) lectures at Bonn University whilst living in Frankfurt.

After listening to Keynes, Drucker concluded that economics was not the primary target for his life's work, as economists were interested in commodities, and he was interested in people. This decision by Drucker should not be interpreted as surrender by him because the subject was beyond his intellect. Any doubt can be dispelled by references to his several times published essays 'Keynes: Economics as a Magical System' first published in 'Virginia Quarterly Review' (Autumn 1946), which with his essay on Kierkegaard, he regarded as his two best works. Also worth noting is his essay 'Schumpeter or Keynes', which was first published in 'Forbes Magazine' (1983).

By Drucker's pursuing his preference of his interest in people, evidence is that the world lost the prospect of an outstanding economist.

Of his other consequential occurrences while in London, he recounted that while sheltering from the rain, he entered an exhibit of Japanese painting. This became a life interest as a collector and advisor to museums, and also as a professorial lecturer on Zen Period Art. By this accident of the weather, he had added another talent to his collection.

**His chance meeting with his wife-to-be**

As his time in London came to end, the most consequential event of his London stay occurred. He married his life-time wife. Their marriage certificate of 16 January 1937 records Drucker as a bachelor whose profession is as a Bank Manager aged twenty-seven. His father Adolf Drucker is a retired civil servant. His wife is Doris Schmitz (born 14 June 1911) aged twenty-five, whose father is Fritz Schmitz, a textile merchant. Doris, having been born in Cologne, Germany, is described as a spinster. Their residence in London was 6b Upper Park Road, Hampstead, London (now No 1 Upper Park Road).

Drucker, an obsessive story teller, described that he first met Doris in Frankfurt when he deputised as a lecturer only to the designated professor's illness. He then continued that they then met by chance in London as each was travelling in opposite directions of the Underground's escalators.

Drucker later concluded that the two best decisions of his life were not embarking on full-time adult education, and not accepting his wife's first refusal of marriage. As a married couple, the Druckers departed for New York to establish a new home in the USA, which would become their adopted country. Their marriage would produce four children, one son and three daughters.

Doris has a doctorate, and has had her own career in addition to being a mother, and ever-dependable wife. She has remained conspicuous in support for her husband and her family's work but mainly inconspicuous in detail. Her book 'Invent Radium or I'll Pull Your Hair' (2004) has provided us with some detail. We now know that her father was a textile merchant who was born in Mainz, and his wife

Clara was a school teacher of secular Jewish stock from East Prussia. When her father joined the German Army in World War I, her family moved to her grandparents' in Mainz. Defeat in the war brought loss of work for her father and privation.

After the privation of war diminished, her later school education progressed with development in literature, music, and a strong interest in physical sports including holidays in Switzerland with different relatives.

School days over, she had a dispute with her mother who insisted that she studied law at university, when Doris's inclination was for science. As an interim measure she was sent to an affluent Anglican household in Tunbridge Wells (Kent, England) as a German Language tutor for their eighteen year old daughter. Doris records that she attended Church with them. After a few weeks her appointment was terminated; after other diversions she enrolled at the London School of Economics on an economics-based course of study and moved into the university's women student accommodation. Part of the condition of the university was that the students had to go into the slums of London to perform social work with impoverished families, and also teach uneducated workers rudimentary education.

Returning home for Christmas, where the festive celebrations were in full swing, she said that she rejected the spirit of goodwill. Resisting yet a further reoccurring attempt by her mother to control her, she left home to return to London to obtain what she describes as the best job she ever had. It was a temporary anthropology research job, and translator for the Warburg Institute of Hamburg. Although an offer came to extend her part-time job, and change her studies from law and economics, to art and art history, she kept her agreement with her mother, and returned to Frankfurt after the two semesters. This meant leaving the London School of Economics during its important formative period of the tenure of Joan Violet Robinson (1903-1983), Lionel Robbins (1898-1984), and Harold Laski (1893-1950), all of whose lectures she attended.

Back in Frankfurt she continued her studies with a compulsory first year course of civil, and criminal administrative law. She found the environment different to the social cohesion of London as the Frankfurt students lived off campus. Also, in contrast the political extreme ultra-left and ultra-right of the Communists and Nazis were marked. Later she reflected that at the time politics had little interest for her, which was a mistake as people like herself should have taken a greater active interest.

Summer found her in Paris as a bank trainee with Rothschild's, which was arranged by her mother through a distant relative. At the start of the new university year she enrolled at The Sorbonne to continue her law studies but struggled to understand the accents of the lecturers. As in London she continued her life experiences but found the French more conservative in their social attitudes to a single woman than in London, until she fell in love with an impoverished artist as her life experiences changed in bohemian Paris. Her time spent in Paris allowed her French to become fluent but her studies suffered. Consequently she enrolled at the conservative Kiel University for a semester, where she caught up with her studies.

Again she returned to Frankfurt to continue her studies, and first met Drucker, who was a more advanced student. She described that they met casually several times. This liaison ended as she commenced what she describes as a dull year from the summer of 1932 in Holland working in a friend's shipping company. *'Peter Drucker was out of my life. We drifted so far apart that I did not even say goodbye to him. How we found each other again is another story.'* (*Ibid*: 2004)

She finished her JD Thesis but did not wish to return to complete further studies, as German Civil Law had been replaced by National Socialism Law. In any event she recalls that she *'would not have been allowed to practise law because of my Jewish ancestors'*.[1]

---

[1] This is a different explanation to that which her husband gives. Drucker gives the reason as not being a German National in his case. The prospect is that her explanation maybe the more likely, although both records may be correct as he is reporting on circumstances six to seven years earlier.

On a long weekend trip to London she found a job as a research assistant to a Mr Barnes, a distinguished professor of international law.

Both she and Drucker tell a similar story of seeing each other on the Piccadilly Underground as they passed on the escalator before stopping to meet; Doris tells that Peter had lost his job at the 'Frankfurter General Anzeiger' and was working in London for an insurance company. She also records that her English was fluent while his was halting. They were drawn together as *'both of us had been cut off from our moorings'* by Hitler's dangerous game plan. Their romance waxed and waned over the next couple of months. After this probationary period the relationship became permanent; she was a market researcher for Marks and Spencer, and described him as being an economist for a merchant bank.

### Their move to America and his 'economic foundation' (1937)

By 1937 they had become disenchanted with Britain's appeasement to Hitler. As noted they married and moved to New York. Shortly after her arrival Doris[2] received an MS in physics from Fairleigh Dickinson

---

[2] As I was drafting this entry I telephoned John Humble and told him that I was including a profile on Doris Drucker in spite of the fact that the profile was of Peter Drucker. John, who worked with Peter Drucker and knew Doris, is the international expert on the application of MbO. He confirmed that it was imperative that Doris was included in essentially a husband and wife team. He said 'I have never been in a

University, and formed a market research business, which she managed for several years. Drucker began working from America as a correspondent for several European newspapers with whom he had previously been commissioned. In America, Drucker found his *workable society* although he would spend the next sixty-eight years suggesting refinements and fundamental adjustments.

It was in America that he crystallised his ideas on what was the third stage of his intellectual journey of discovery of his ethical *purpose for living*, that of evolving his ideas on what he perceived as the driving force of society, its Economics. To arrive at his economic ideas, he considered the works of his predecessors.

He attributes that economic man was recognised by Adam Smith (1723-1790) and that he was of Smith's past era. He returned to Marx and identified the fault-line in his economics of regarding the worker as the economic force, and rejecting that it was someone else's capital that paid for the machines, equipment and power, while ignoring the input of management, all to the creation of Marx's surplus-value.

Hitler's economics, he considered, were built on a war-economy where the population were told that they must prepare for war as the country was under imminent threat of attack. For Drucker, it was the reverse

---

household that had so much brain power'.

of this situation as the Nazis always intended to be the aggressor. However, for him, the greatest abhorrence was the persecution of minorities who were used as the blame factor for the hardships in people's economic lives. One positive economics idea of Hitler's did eventually find use with Drucker. It was that of *privatisation*. When Hitler came to power the Weimar economy was in a state of collapse. Drucker described that Hitler, who wanted only power and control, had to become involved in management and rescue the failing banks. Similarly though not mentioned by Drucker, coalmines and heavy industry were also rescued. Drucker continued that once the banks had been stabilised they were returned to private ownership, which he first described as re-privatisation.

Keynes he regarded as an outstanding intellect but considered his economic ideas as old-fashioned and a contributor to, rather than a solver of, the economic problems. For Drucker, Keynes' basic theories were that the economy had to be adjusted to bring it back to his goal of equilibrium, which Drucker described as Keynes making adjustments to his master plan by applying 'his pedals'. Drucker continued that Keynes was wrong to ignore productivity as a variable, and explained that once Keynes had ascertained the output forecast from the manufacturing sector, he treated them as fixed, and took no account of increased outputs through greater productivity. Keynes, for Drucker, also had a similar fixed opinion on consumers, who Keynes believed acted as he predicted. Drucker's position was opposite, as he maintained that productivity was the foundation of economics, and that as consumers people were irrationally unpredictable, which they were entitled to be, as only the customers could determine what value was for themselves.

Where Drucker did support Keynes was for his proposal at the Bretton Wood Conference of 1944, of creating the Bancor as the new international reserve currency to give monetary stability to the participating countries. That it was not adopted resulted in the later international financial crisis, which Drucker believed could have been averted if the Bancor has been established.

Having rejected the totalitarian economics of Marx, and Hitler, and the interventionist programmed economics of Keynes; Drucker confirmed that the economics of his father's friend, Joseph Aloisius Julius Schumpeter (1883-1950) was the correct one.

Schumpeter started from the position that the economy is in equilibrium only in the transition period when the economy travels from its two extremes of contraction to expansion. For Schumpeter the economy behaves in waves. At the bottom of the economic activity in the most extreme cases a depression occurs. At this juncture governments should borrow only to protect the members of society who do not have the capacity to protect themselves, as in extreme occurrences as wars and major financial banking dislocations.

With this foundation in place Schumpeter postulates that when the economy is in the trough, the entrepreneurs emerge after perceiving opportunities. They apply innovation and start new combinations (ventures). By their activity the economy recovers as more entrepreneurs join in, thus creating prosperity. When the economy recovery reaches the crest of the wave, the entrepreneurs realise that the opportunities have disappeared, so consequently they refrain from promoting new ventures. The result is that the economic activity contracts and the economy corrects its excessive activity, and declines down the wave pattern towards the trough.

It is at the crest that Schumpeter warned that governments always make the mistake of interceding to dampen the activity. For him, this was a fundamental error because intervention correction was not needed, as correction was naturally happening. By their interventions governments accelerated the natural patterns in the market, and cause depressions. It was the pattern of expansion and contraction that Schumpeter termed 'creative destruction'. Another essential of Schumpeter's argument as to why the economy could never be in permanent equilibrium, which set him at odds with Keynes, was that he believed that productivity was an essential variable in the economy. Also he believed that people were unpredictable in their purchasing decisions. They had a right to, and did, behave irrationally, in other people's judgement, in selecting what they believed was value when they considered a purchase. Both of these last two variables Keynes believed he could forecast.

Regarding public borrowings Schumpeter believed budgets should be balanced except in exceptional times. Keynes believed that public borrowing was a component to keep the economy in equilibrium with lending in recessions and claw-back in recovery. What Keynes never told us was what happened if the international currency markets stopped lending to the borrowing countries. Drucker agreed with all of these arguments of Schumpeter; where they differed was that Schumpeter believed that entrepreneurial opportunities were diminishing, while Drucker believed that they were growing, but were different.

Of Keynes' economics, Drucker terms them as the economics of depression based upon his argument that if you pump money into the economy in a recession the poor still do not have any money, while the wealthy take the opportunity to pay off their debts, rather than spend, and help the economy to recover. For Keynes, money saved was capital destroyed, whereas for Schumpeter and Drucker it was capital held in reserve. Although Schumpeter disagreed with Keynes for his economic theories, he credited him with being an outstanding intellectual.

The common denominators of Drucker, Keynes and Schumpeter were that *laissez-faire* economics were the thing of the past; that they anticipated their economics functioning only in a democratic society. Of their attitudes towards statisticians, Keynes complained in the early 1920s that there was insufficient information in the civil service upon which to accurately construct his models, while Schumpeter and Drucker both had a cynical distrust of them, believing that they could be constructed to support the answer required.

**His life in America**

Returning to Drucker's life, he was now settled in New York, while his career as a journalist expanded into articles and papers for quality magazines and journals. By May 1939 he had published his first major book 'The End of Economic Man', which was conceived in 1933 when Hitler came to power. He described it as an *'attempt to analyse the roots of Nazism and the decay of Europe's liberal and humanist traditions'* (Drucker 1979). The book is an audit of events, ideas, and personalities that went back to Ancient Greece, progressed through Medieval Christianity compared the eighteenth-century differences of the development of the English parliamentary system with the French Revolution, and their respective formative thinkers, to arrive at *'the despair of the masses'* in Germany, brought about by economic and ethical collapse. He reflects on the German/Russian alliance and concludes that Hitler's irrationality is a characteristic that could destroy the alliance, which it did. Marx is prominent. The economist Adam Smith is mentioned for identifying economic man of the mercantile age, while Keynes is linked to the American Irvine Fisher (1867-1947) of Yale for denying the components of the Depression.[3] What the book is conveying is the method of his later books, as he builds an interlocking pattern of ideas holistically. The book is pessimistic as it regards the prospects of the remainder of democratic Europe falling under totalitarian rule as being high, while also predicting in the long term that totalitarian rule could not survive. America is regarded as exceptionally different, and the only hope, with Henry Ford (1863-1947) mentioned as a free enterprise contributor. Also on what will eventually become Drucker's discovery of management, Ford and Walther Rathenau (1867-1922), the German polymath and industrialist, are included, together with the Welshman Robert Owen (1771-1858) who is described as, *'that almost saintly figure of early capitalism'* for his earlier democratic ideas of factory employment. Although America will face threats, its basic structure provides a *workable society*. Amongst the book's reviewers was Winston Churchill (1874-1965) in the 'Times Literary Supplement' (1939).

By 1941 Drucker had returned to his teaching career at Sarah Lawrence College in Bronxville, New York and was teaching economics, and statistics one day a week. Later in 1941 he began teaching at Benning

---

[3] See 'The Forgotten Man' Amity Shlaes (2007) New York: Harper Collins, which links Keynes and Fisher's role in the economics of the Depression. Shlaes supports Drucker's analysis.

College Vermont, on a weekly basis, together with lecturing as a visitor at other small colleges throughout America. As America entered the war in 1941, he had lectured in fifty such colleges. In the summer of 1942 he had taken up a full-time appointment at Bennington, where he taught subjects on demand. He said that he wanted to keep on teaching whatever subject was needed as he taught American government, history, literature, religion, economics, political theory, philosophy and management. Early in his stay at Bennington he became an American citizen, and remained at the college as Professor of Politics and Philosophy until 1945.

Coincidentally, with an increase in the numbers of quality journals to which he was a contributor, Drucker's second book 'The Future of Industrial Man' (1942) was published. Its tone is optimistic, as he tells his audience that they must plan for their world after Hitler's defeat.

The book embraces his ideas on Christian ethics, and expands on his 'free society and free government', while giving an historical lesson on the evolution of society. He reinforces his ideas that society must provide the individual with <u>Freedom</u>, <u>Status</u>, and <u>Function</u>. He argues that the mercantile society is a society of the past, with output equating to established demands; also that the mass society of the agrarian society had been eclipsed by the industrial society, which had not yet developed into a working society.

The agrarian society had meant that the family was one economic integrated unit, where each member was dependent on the other's contributions. Now with the industrial age, families were dispersed and lost mutual identity. Families were becoming disconnected, the consequence of which he prophetically forecast would lead to a new pattern of divorces, which it did.

What emerged from this book was the solution as to how the industrial society would be brought about. Influenced by Rathenau he proposed that the corporation (the large commercial organisation) should be the basis of the new *'local self-governing industrial community…'*, which would replace centralised bureaucracy. For the workers in the industrial society to function, it is as a member of the 'plant' through which they will gain status, and function, in a free and functioning industrial society. It was an idea that he laboured with for over a decade under amended titles, but which failed to find mass appeal. Eventually he gave up the struggle, and commented that it was his best idea that never worked.[4]

---

[4] Drucker ultimately found an exception *plant* community in 'The Ecological Vision' (1993: 55) New Brunswick USA; Transition Publishers London: Drucker explains that Thomas Watson Snr at IBM created the 'plant community' *'He created in the 1930s the social organisation, the work community of the post industrial age'*. Thomas Watson Snr was influenced by John Henry Patterson (1844 -1922) the founder of NCR which became IBM. See Patterson's biography – 'John. H. Patterson. Pioneer in Industrial Welfare' Crowther.S (1926) New York Garden City Printing Company.

Another of Rathenau's ideas he used was that management had eclipsed the power of the owners of the business, the shareholders. He also credits Adolf Augustus Berle (1895-1971) and Gardiner Coit Means (1896-1988), who followed and expanded on Rathenau's ideas, with their book 'The Modern Corporation and Private Property' (1933). Drucker, while praising managers for their essential contribution to society, felt management had to be made into a constitutionally legitimate force to comply with the basic requirement of a free society which was that power had to be answerable to the members of society. Again he laboured for several decades but never found a convincing answer for himself. Eventually he concluded that it had become an accepted part of society by usage.

In contrast Drucker drew attention to James Burnham's (1905-1987) book 'The Managerial Revolution' (1941), which Drucker described as creating great interest in America. Burnham argues that management power is legitimate and that it will inevitably lead to a managerial society. Drucker argues that the argument of legitimacy is similar to those projected by Nazism and Communism, and that the consequence of accepting Burnham's arguments would be that all industrial countries will become totalitarian. Of the management society that Burnham forecast, it had been the society for the first third of the twentieth-century, and is already a thing of the past.

Drucker's interest in management was now being established as he identified *decentralisation* as a structure and the desirable pattern for 'big businesses in a free enterprise society'. Schumpeter is mentioned by name for the first time in Drucker's books as having '*the only constituent and effective contemporary theory of capitalisation*'. This is centred on 'private initiative' – the enterprising manager. It is the manager who is productive, with capital being a subordinate part. '*Schumpeter is hard pressed to find a convincing justification for capital's claims to a share in the profit*'. What Schumpeter proposed was that the surplus value, the profit, was management's.

What has emerged is that Drucker is having further thoughts on his original intellectual journey. His Ethics have their established position. His Society as the order that provides the social environment for life has been identified. His Economics is now being reconsidered as the third and final part of man's workable habitat. What is emerging is a reassessment that economics is the concluding part of that habitat. What Drucker is realising is that although economics is an essential part of the total habitat it is only a theory that has to be the correct selection for society to fulfil its essential promise of prosperity. The consequence of this choice is the difference between depression and prosperity. His new recognition is that it is management that is the driving force that creates economic value, productivity and prosperity. This is his new personal discovery, which became the fourth part of his intellectual journey of discovery for his *purpose for living*, as he mentions Andrew Carnegie (1835-1919), J Pierpont Morgan (1837-1913), John D

45

Rockefeller (1839-1937), and James Watt (1736-1819). Owen D Young (1874-1962) of General Electric is identified as one of the new breed of professional managers who were not proprietors.

Frederick Winslow Taylor (1856-1915) is introduced as making it possible for organising the worker to operate similarly to a machine. Drucker's subsequent treatment of Taylor is a process of metamorphosis. He credits him with making the treatment of work possible, for separating work from its planning. He then links him to the patterns of the totalitarian controller of the inter-World Wars I & II years. He rehabilitates him for anticipating Automation, the new integration of work, before concluding that he changed the way we manage, by making the measurement of work possible. Eventually in the age of the knowledge worker he concludes that although Taylor separated work from its planning, Drucker reflects that he did not say that the two processes had to be carried out by different people.

Drucker's book received complimentary reviews from rated intellectuals as Jacques Barzun (1907-   ). By the time that the book was published, Drucker's career was developing rapidly; he began broadcasting, was lecturing extensively, and expanding the range of the quality publications to which he was a contributor.

Having aroused his own interest in management, he turned his attention to discover what it was. His literary research revealed shelves of books on the functions of management, with little material that gave an overview. Attempts to advance his own research into major corporations met with rejections, as he said that he was seen as a dangerous radical.

**His break into management**

As he was on the verge of abandoning his quest, he received a call in late 1943 from General Motors (GM), then the world's largest corporation with its five hundred thousand employees. The caller told him they had read his latest book, and invited him to conduct a study into their operations. This was the opportunity that Drucker was seeking. He was seconded from Bennington for his project, and he was given free access to GM's locations. His object was to study GM as a social organisation. The work resulted in the management education that Drucker needed as he discovered management for himself, as is recorded in his first book on management 'Concept of the Corporation' (1946). It is a comprehensive catalogue of the functions and activities of management, some of which he described in detail, while others only receive a by-line. Comparisons of his listings with his later works reveal that he was setting a large part of the basic agenda for his lifetime writing on the subject.

For Drucker, the strength of the organisation was dependent upon the quality of the chief executive. Fortunately GM had an outstanding leader in Alfred Pritchard Sloan Jnr (1875-1966). What Drucker observed was that there was never any doubt that Mr Sloan was the chief (CEO), but he made it clear through his practice that strategic discussions of the corporations were the job of the chief executive with his small competent team, which had distinctive duties. It was only the executive team's job to set the strategy of the organisation; consequently the quality of their decisions affected the fate of the corporation. Such was the importance of the quality of the decisions in general that Sloan was known to abandon meetings and board meetings if sufficient dissent had not occurred. His reasoning was that essential decisions had to be the correct ones, which were determined only by vigorous examination. Drucker exposed many essential activities within GM. Amongst those that he found important was Sloan's marketing strategy of having a range of marques which introduced new car models annually to stimulate demand. He also recognised that GM were also in the second-hand car market, as the customers for their new models had to be able to sell their existing car to be able to trade-up, and purchase the new models. Sloan was adamant that market competition was essential to measure if the corporate performance was fulfilling its productive intentions.

One of the other salient observations that Drucker made was the identification of Sloan's deputy Frank Donaldson Brown (1885-1965), who had worked on the development of the accounting procedure of

Return on Investment (ROI), first at Du Pont in the 1900s and then at GM. The application of ROI allowed internal charges to be subjected to objective cost performance. What it made possible was that inter-divisional charges could be judged against market competition standards rather than on a cost-plus basis. This idea Drucker would develop into his own idea of 'activity accounting' which was acknowledged by Robert Kaplan and David Norton as the foundations for their own 'Balanced Scorecard' (1992).

The second salient observation was that Drucker described how Sloan's *decentralisation* as a corporate-delegated structure worked. This description preceded Alfred Du Pont Chandler Jnr's (1918-2007) 'Strategy and Structure' (1962).

Of 'Concept' over half of its content is devoted to Drucker's own ideas on issues that he perceived GM should address. He believed that the workers' interests should be more at the forefront of GM policies as he developed his ideas on his 'self-governing plant community', which would give the workers a role in managing their own cafeterias, welfare, and shift allocations. He drew attention to the worker's dread of 'the demon' of unemployment, and their frustration, at what he saw were shrinking opportunities for advancement. He examined the foreman's role, which was then ambiguous, as he was neither worker nor manager. His conclusion was that he was a manager, and should be recognised as such.

The labour unions, he considered, were an indisputable third part of the industrial society organisation, together with managers and workers. His engagement with the role of the labour unions occupied his time for the remainder of the 1950s as he tried to find a constructive role for them. Eventually he concluded that they became a force against society with their rights to strike, which he supported in principle, when they disrupted ordinary citizens' lives who were not a party to the dispute.

The outcome of Drucker's work was that the research, which was never intended to be a book but an internal report, was by agreement published as 'Concept of the Corporation' (1946).[5] Despite defining the need for corporations to make adequate profits to survive, GM were offended by the book as Sloan believed that Drucker was suggesting that they embark on a social agenda, which he considered was the government's, not the corporation's, responsibility. This coincided with the time when GM had a more than large enough agenda to manage their own business as their plans to reorganise from war prioritised output, to that of a civilian society, resulted in the labour unions embarking on a bitter one-hundred-and-thirteen day strike. As Drucker's book was published during the middle of this battle, it only added to GM's sensitivities.

---

[5] Its British title was 'Big Business' because the publishers did not believe that the British readers would understand what Corporation meant.

As for academic reviewers, as it was categorised as neither society nor economics, the purpose of the book was misunderstood. It was suggested that Drucker had destroyed a promising academic career, which resulted in the academic society ceasing to issue their invitations. This attitude was in contrast to the market reaction which embraced his work, especially the American service personnel returning from the war to construct a civilian life. The popularity of the book was aided by one of the government's initiative the 'GI Bill of Rights', which provided advanced education for the demobbed in what John E Flaherty (1999) described as 'the most spectacular and daring venture in the history of education' as two and one third million signed up for the scheme. As the troops returned from the war, many wanted to know about big business and how it worked. Drucker's book was waiting to tell them, not only how GM worked, but he introduced them to the wider management ideas of Chester Irvine Barnard (1886-1961), James David Mooney (1884-1957), Ordway Tead (1891-1973), and the Harvard Business School, who with their writings had all contributed to the understanding of the corporation as an organisation. Also introduced was John Llewellyn Lewis (1880-1969), the disruptive labour union leader. Carried forward were the previously mentioned Burnham, Schumpeter, Adam Smith, Taylor and the Tennessee Valley Authority Scheme (TVA).

For the returning troops it introduced them to management; for Drucker it launched him on a further adaptation of his career as a writer on management with one of his best selling books that has been regularly reprinted to meet demand. It is now acknowledged as the first book that examined the industrial corporation as being a 'social organisation'.

With his career as a management thinker launched, Drucker continued, and produced his next book, 'The New Society' (1950). This coincided with his moving back to New York as Professor of Management at its University's Graduate Business School. The book is a tidying and expansion of some of his ideas from (Drucker 1946) of the dilemma of the labour unions; worker's satisfaction; law of higher output; 'the plant community'; that decentralisation is the best structure; attitudes to profit, and avoidance of losses. His society is neither capitalist nor socialist. While accepting that market force is the correct solution for serving the consumer's best interest, it is not the solution for all projects — especially those with a high potential for social disruption as Roosevelt's New Deal, Depression-correcting TVA Scheme, which was, and should be, managed under government direction and control.

Developing his economics he introduced Eugen von Böhm-Bawerk (1851-1914), founder of the Austrian School, and attributed one of his theories of uncertainty as the foundation of a management idea that increased output was not always the best policy if increased sales did not follow. Frank Hyneman Knight (1885-1972) of the Chicago School was linked with Schumpeter for progressing towards an adequate theory of industrial economics. Drucker also drew attention to Karl Polanyi's (1886-1964) 'The Great Transformation' (1944), [6] and agreed with him that a market that provided only for status without function would inevitably collapse.

Of management ideas, Drucker noted that the industrial enterprise was a social institution, an old idea that dates from the French 'Romantic Socialites' of the early eighteenth-century. Of current work he noted that there were too many modern studies for him to catalogue as he mentioned the Australian Elton George Mayo (1880-1949) for American's best known Hawthorne Investigations and the American Edward Wright Bakke (1903-1971) for his first-hand study as he intentionally lived in the same impoverished conditions as the British unemployed workers in London, to gather information about its effect, and its resulting consequences for this doctoral thesis.

As Drucker developed his ideas on management he called for a managerial attitude from all the members of the organisation, but maintained that only the managers 'must manage'. Only the managers were responsible for deciding the answer to the question 'what business is the enterprise really in'? Also it was the manager's

---

[6] Polanyi introduced Drucker to Keynes on Drucker's return from Hamburg to Vienna, Christmas 1928.

responsibility to organise the enterprise's human resources for their efficient use, and to plan for the orderly success in top management.

People were again central to his work with workers wanting involvement, and opportunities, which was becoming more difficult to provide as mass-production had separated 'the worker from the product'. That management was failing to address these issues was why the labour unions appealed to the workers. That many of the labour union leaders were primarily interested in their own self-promotion and racketeering was adding to the workers' perception of neglect. Aldous Huxley's (1894-1963) 'Brave New World' (1932) and Charlie Chaplin's (1889-1977) film 'Modern Times' (1936) were quoted to support the worker's frustration.

Drucker accepted the expectations from the workers that a wage guarantee would be desirable. He concluded that only the large employers could provide an internal scheme with about a one-third income guarantee. Although Procter and Gamble had a much admired internal scheme Drucker argued that unless the scheme was insurance guaranteed, then with the commercial risk of bankruptcy, company schemes could never be fully guaranteed.[7]

---

[7] Drucker would later warn managers of the day not to commit the organisation to some long-term liability that was not sustainable. See GM's government bail-out from failure through it long-term internal unfundable social benefit promises to its workforce - summer 2009.

Of the question 'what business is the enterprise really in'? Drucker returned to and made clear it was the first question the "top team" needed to ask itself. He concluded that it sounded a simple question but was often a difficult question to answer.[8]

Though a moderate compared with John L. Lewis, Philip Murray (1886-1962) of the steelworkers' union suggested the creation of a social fund to protect workers displaced by new technology. Drucker rejected this as protecting jobs that didn't exist. He concluded that the resistance to increase in productivity was a similar problem to that of the wage conflict.

Drucker also discussed 'equal opportunities' (which did not have today's meaning of protection against sexism and the interest of minority groups). Its context was questioning the impact of improved university education on recruitment of middle, and upper management applicants who were receiving preference to people from the shop floor, including those who had made foreman grade. Drucker regarded this pattern as not acceptable and importantly Drucker made his first announcement on innovation and entrepreneurship. 'The abilities which make for scholastic success are not the abilities the enterprise need. By asking the school master to pick management, the enterprise

---

[8] An example would be an airline; are they flying planes, or satisfying customers' transport, and for what purpose?

will deny the very men it needs most: the entrepreneur, the innovator, the risk-taker.' (Page:173)

The reviews of this book were supportive in general, although some had different ideas from his on his social and political selections, as would be expected. Personally Drucker was in full stride with his writing, management consulting, and his lecturing well-established.

## His answer to management – 'Management by Objective and Self-Control' (MbO)

That he had matured into an outstanding management thinker is confirmed in his next book 'The Practice of Management' (1954), which has support for being the best book on management ever written. He describes it as explaining what management is, and how managers do their jobs. It launches his Management by Objectives and Self Control (MbO) on the world.

He tells his audience that *'the manager is the dynamic, life giving element in every business'* that:

> *'The emergence of management as an essential, a distinct and a leading institution is a pivotal event in social history. Rarely, if ever, has a new basic institution, a new leading group, emerged as fast as has management since the turn of his century. Rarely, in human history has a new*

*institution proven indispensable so quickly; and even less often has a new institution arrived with so little opposition, so little disturbance, so little controversy'*. (*Ibid*:3)

Also he states that there is only one valued definition of business purpose: '*to create a customer*' to which he later added '*and get paid*'.

The book is rooted in his experience and uses circa one hundred and ten case studies. The book emerges from a commission of a management practice review team for General Electric of America (GE) commissioned by the CEO Ralph Jerron Cordiner (1900-1973) of which Drucker was an original member and eventually its leader. Drucker worked closely with Harold Francis Smiddy (1900-1978) who was the initial leader and who wrote a set of Blue Book volumes for GE's use as a project record.

Of Drucker's case studies, IBM, Sears and GE receive the best recommendations, while Ford, Drucker's earliest foreign industrial business influence, is relegated as a non-contemporary manager, who has failed to adequately delegate through not having an appropriate structure. IBM scores for the best integration of labour and customer service attitude; Sears, for the quality of its succession policies for its CEOs, and GE, for the quality and depth of its management in the most complex multi-division business. For Drucker, within all organisations there will be a common set of functions. Although all will be present, their value and priority will change from time to time. Consequently, they will have to be re-evaluated against each other. This is anticipating the later idea of the 'balanced scorecard'.

Drucker identifies a new type of worker who is neither management nor labour. It is the professional workers who have split loyalties, believing their employer and upholding their professional standards.

The book's text and its 'Selected Bibliography' is a catalogue of who are the most consequential management thinkers in practice, or academia, in America, and Europe.

From the book emerge nine key ideas.

- Management will be Management by Objectives and Self-Control (MbO), which is a system where the targets are agreed *'It ensures performances by converting objective needs into personal goals. And this is genuine freedom and freedom under the law'.*[9]
- Decentralisation is the preferred structure, although task-force groups within are appropriate for special projects.
- Integration of productivity by Automation is the new way of working, for profit.
- Managers must measure.
- The entrepreneurial functions are marketing and innovation.
- People are central to the organisation.
- The manager's job is total integration after deciding 'what business are we in'? They manage themselves, other managers, workers and work. They need teamwork.
- Delegation is by Span of Control for low trained grade members (one manager for five manual workers) or by Span

---

[9] Of Smiddy's work, Drucker recognised the essentiality of his idea as part of MbO; that team members should write to their managers every six months, a letter setting out what their personal contribution should be to the objectives of the organisation for the following period. The letter should also confirm what the team member expected from their manager and from other parts of the organisation.

On receipt of the letter the manager and the team member met and agreed and confirmed their commitment.

The consequence of this letter is that when the sequence is complete every member of the organisation knows what their objectives are, and can access for themselves, if they are being attained without being reminded by others.

> of Managerial Responsibility for high trained grade members (one manager to eighty intellectual workers – later *'knowledge workers'*).
> - Time is always a manager's constraint.
> - Rejected is 'staff and line' management.

Such is the range of new ideas in the book, its contents can only be given justice by a full-study. Only a selection of his ideas can be included.

As people are central to Drucker's ideas there is justification in selecting an example on people from the book's contents on motivation. Drucker's basic and consistent theory is that without the co-operation and contribution of people nothing takes place. On the understanding of the motivation of people he joins with Douglas Murray McGregor (1906-1964) whose ideas had developed simultaneously. McGregor had two positions; Theory 'X', which postulates that people did not want to work: Theory 'Y' is that they did. Drucker agreed with Theory 'Y' on the grounds that if people did not want to work then the manager's job was impossible (McGregor 1960). Also, while supporting McGregor, Drucker coins the term 'Human Resources' (Marciano 1995) as he begins a prolonged criticism of Personnel Administration, which he believed concentrated on the wrong priorities as he asks 'Is Personnel Management Bankrupt'? He recommends the articles and papers of Thomas Gardiner Spates (1890-

1988) from the early 1920s, which contain every thing that is in today's big text books except a chapter on union relations. The work of psychiatrists Sir Cyril Ludowic Burt (1883-1971) and Hugo Münsterberg (1863-1916) has by now been included.

Similarly to Drucker's interest in people, he sees marketing as one of the organisation's essentials. Cyrus Hall McCormick (1809-1884), who invented the reaper combine harvester and other farm machinery, is identified as the 'Father of Marketing' because he not only designed a product which the farmers wanted, but also a full set of marketing and sales practices for a completely new industry. In the process he revolutionized agriculture, including methods of finance, so that the farmers could buy the equipment.

As a foretaste of what had become Drucker's encyclopaedic knowledge of management he summarises Scientific Management beginning in 1885 with Taylor, who was joined by Henry Laurence Gantt (1861-1919) and the Gilbreths, Frank Bunker (1863-1926), and Lillian Evelyn Möller (1878-1972), in America, while independently in France, Henri Jules Fayol (1841-1925) CEO of a major mining company, developed executive management practices. Drucker notes that since the work of these pioneers oceans of papers have been reproduced with few new concepts, excepting by Lillian Gilbreth and Harry Arthur Hopf (1882-1949).[10]

---

[10] To summarise, Taylor provided work study, which enabled work to be planned, and

As an overview, Drucker observes that even good ideas have to be communicated to be effective. He references William Barnes Given Jnr's (1886-1968) book 'Bottom Up Management' (1949), which as its title suggests, communication should be from the bottom of the organisation upwards – 'bottom-up'. This idea Drucker totally rejects as he maintained that communications had to be in all directions.

Ducker adds to his earlier ideas on economics as he comments on Schumpeter: 'Readers familiar with the work of Joseph A Schumpeter will recognise without special reference how much the author owes to this most fruitful of modern economists' (*Ibid*:vii-viii). Economists now doubt that there are business cycles. Even Schumpeter 'laboured mightily for twenty-five years to find the *cycle*'. Because there are 'so many different cyclical movements' 'it can only be analysed *in retrospect*' which is of little use in managing a business.

---

measured (timed) where people were paid on output. Gantt refined the system by allowing people adaption time while they learnt their new tasks. Gantt's unique contribution is that he revolutionised the planning of work. He devised the 'Gantt Chart' or 'Bar Chart', which incorporated into a single sheet, what had taken thirty-seven different curve charts for its predecessor to convey. It made possible the plotting of output against time. It was the fore-runner of the further innovations of planning of 'Critical Path', and PERT - 'programme evaluation and research techniques'.

Frank Gilbreth devised 'motion study', which eliminated unnecessary movements in the sequences of work. His aim was to take fatigue out of work. Lillian applied psychology to work, and added a personal emphasis. Fayol laid down the foundation of the functions of management as planning, organising, motivating, and coordinating. Hopf followed the original pioneers. Where they had concentrated on manual work, Hopf applied a more modern form of scientific management to clerical work.

Also, it was Drucker (1954) who recognised the centrality of economics more than his contemporary management theorists, in identifying new contributing economists, such as Joel Dean (1906-1979) for his business management economics together with Malcolm Perrine McNair (1894-1985) for his advertising economics; Simon Smith Kuznets (1901-1985), who showed a direct relationship between capital equipment, and productivity; and George Katona (1901-1981) who had linked psychological behaviour to customer's purchasing patterns.

As we examine Drucker's work we are likely to come across unexpected surprises which are ideas that you are unlikely to find in the work of other management writers. Writing of managers, Drucker warns against '*safe mediocrity*' because "*the first requirement of management spirit is high demand on performance*". Drucker's advice against safe mediocrity is that — "*Nobody learns except by making mistakes as it is the essential part of learning by the manager for the top-level job*". Why it is essential is that in "*not having made mistakes he will not have learned how to spot them early and how to correct them*". (1954:145)

Of the reviews, all were positive with some rave reviews such as: 'One of the most outstanding contributions to management theory and practice that has been published in the English language'.

With the foundation of his management ideas established, his pattern of writing had also been set. Of his total of the equivalent of forty books written over sixty-five years, one is autobiographical, two are novels, and the remainder are divided between management, and economics, politics, and society. Some of his books have a complex range of ideas; others have a single message, which sometimes are refinements on statements from the past which become in effect, his latest thesis.

## His next batch of ideas

As Drucker moved on, his next book was 'America's Next Twenty Years' (1955). That it is still overlooked is a loss, as it was way ahead of its time. It was probably the first exposition in management writing where he sets the precedent for using demographics for forecasting future trends for businesses.

'Landmarks of Tomorrow' (1959) follows as he continues to develop and add variations on his previous themes, and also tells us that *'social innovation is nothing new'* as we could not dream of an industrial economy without the seventeenth-century innovation of insurance for risks. The new need is for people with education, who are the most advanced form of capital investment. On management ideas he warns that *there is an all-too-common belief that planning eliminates risks'*. It is the most dangerous delusion of all, since planning is actually risk-taking and risk-creating. Of the business *'every theory eventually becomes obsolete'*. The danger is that the attitude to question one's success is one of the rarest insights. All too often this crucial review is taken too late, after the company has started to go downhill.

On the environment, although we have not yet built a solar energy plan, GE has proved it is possible. Of new opportunities, biological energy is now becoming possible and aqua-culture is a development area with more food from the sea. Later he will suggest we should be paying a full replacement cost, as we deplete natural resources.

On an international front, his interest in Japan is confirmed as the publication of the book coincides with his joining the American advisors to Japan, who include William Edwards Deming (1900-1993) and Joseph Moses Juran (1904-2008). Drucker's advice to the Japanese is that they must westernise to survive. Such will become Drucker's success in Japan with business leaders that he will become the equivalent of a national treasure.

Also for the first time Drucker discusses 'Gestalt'.

> *'These are all concepts of a whole, of a pattern or of a configuration which can be understood as a whole. It is at the "centre of our economic life, the business enterprise." None of those are new concepts… namely that the parts exist in contemplation of the whole'.*

What we are seeing in Drucker's work is a pattern of swinging from his management writing to society, politics, and economic, with a new distinctive style of writing on management. Many of the points that he makes are very clearly illustrated, sometimes by parables, or with the recollection of a story as both are used as cameos that link his ideas together. Drucker continues that management is rooted not only in the manager's technical functions, but also in the world that it operates within, politically, socially, locally and internationally. All of the time he is making his audience think, as he sends clear messages telling them that inside the business are only costs. The rewards are outside in the market. What Drucker is describing to the manager is a different world to the one that they thought they were operating within.

As his work progresses he builds a catalogue of management ideas that eventually accumulate to a catalogue of almost all of the worthwhile messages. Even the ones that he was not the originator of, he is one of the earliest to acknowledge.

His next book 'Managing For Results' (1964) is a book that he wanted to call 'strategy' but his publishers rejected the idea on the grounds that his audience would not understand what it meant.

The book is one of the first books on strategic market analysis. He tells the managers that the customers buy only what they believe is value, not what the business thinks it is selling: *'There is only one person who really knows: the customer'*. He continues that no business can do everything; they must build on their strengths. In other's hands this later became 'stick to your knitting' (Peters & Waterman 1982) or 'core competences' (Hamel & Prahalad 1990).

He classifies the business' products, and identifies five classifications:

1. Today's breadwinners
2. Tomorrow's breadwinners
3. Productive specialities
4. Development products
5. Failures

and shows managers how to analyses their potential, and dangers.

He also produces a programme for performance where he sets down the manager's tasks. Just as the manager had believed that he had conquered the job, he then tells them that they will have to diligently, energetically and continually measure targets against reality, and make the necessary adjustments.

The impression left is that if managers were made to read this book before embarking on their careers, many would choose another profession. Schumpeter made the point that he could not see why people wanted to be a manager — it took too much effort.

'Managing for Results' (1964) was followed by a calmer book, 'The Effective Executive' (1966). This is a handbook for managers to keep in their desk as it is an *aide-memoire* to help them focus on their tasks and self-organise. The book reinforces some of his earlier ideas as he is warning on statistics. He makes the point that when someone sets out to prove a point, they can always find figures to prove their target. Of his new ideas, he coins the phrase *knowledge workers*, the new major resource. They are new production factors in the developed countries where they have replaced the manual worker. He also introduces the term *executive* into his work for the first time as he describes *knowledge workers* as 'all being' executives. When he describes '*Such a man (or woman) must make decisions*' he is identifying women for the first time as executives, and managers. Lillian Gilbreth was previously included as a management pioneer.


He summarises his directions to managers, as effectiveness must be learned. It is the managers' job and what they are paid for. He claims that his book is the first word on the subject of effectiveness, which is to '*get the right things done*', whereas efficiency is doing the right thing. The tasks are to build on the strengths of oneself and the organisation to make them productive while eliminating weakness. Effectiveness comes from concentration of efforts by making the best decisions based upon information. Decision-making is a judgement of a choice between alternatives and rarely between right and wrong. Effectiveness relies on teamwork, good human relations, aided by developing people. He recommends that amongst the main aids the manager should use Programme Evaluation and Review Technique (PERT) Analysis. He asked himself the questions '*will the computer change all this.*' '*The computer is a potent tool… but unlike the wheel or saw it cannot do anything a man cannot do – although it can do many things faster'.* Although it cannot make strategic decisions, it can help by providing information. The final sentence of the book for the manager is 'effectiveness *must* be learned'.[11]

Having written two books on management, Drucker swings back to his alternative theme of politics, society, economics and ethics. Classifying Drucker has for many produced a problem that they have not resolved. Trying to be helpful when he later described himself as a *'social ecologist'* he described his writing as divided into two main groupings. In reality, every book that Drucker wrote always had some message relevant to the manager.

This interweave of ideas is graphically apparent in his next book 'The Age of Discontinuity: Guidelines to our Changing Society' (1969). While Drucker makes reference to some of his older ideas, and relates to the past, his underlying message is that the manager's world is not in a temporary disturbance that will soon revert to its previous patterns, but that it has changed, and will continue to change for ever. Kierkegaard is again referenced as the only one to ask *'how is human existence possible?'*. Marx is mentioned for his failed society, and economics. On Keynes, Drucker maintains his previous conclusions

---

[11] In 1996 'The Effective Executive, Managing for Results', and 'Innovation and Entrepreneurship' (1985) were reissued in a collected volume 'The Executive in Action'.

with only the Bancor receiving credit as he finds a flaw in his conflict of protecting what we already have, and requiring further growth. Schumpeter is again credited for identifying that the economic growth is caused by the entrepreneur as its agent. Kuznets is again mentioned and is identified as supporting Schumpeter's sixty-year idea that knowledge alone, rather than capital, creates productivity. Apart from drawing on new modern contributions, Drucker also draws upon the past, including Aquinas, Socrates and Zola.

Of the modern world *lifetime learning* is added to the *knowledge worker* in a world that has become a global shopping zone, with global money. He is having doubt about decentralisation being the only effective structure, as he extends his ideas to include team working, which he compares with jazz-combos, where each player improvises, yet maintains the group's confidence that they are contributing to the end result. Similarly in management teams of diverse disciplines, they make their own specialist contribution, which is only generally understood by their colleagues, yet all have confidence that it is relevant to the end result of the task-force team.

Drucker identified that new opportunities were emerging which challenged the manager's markets. He recognised that manufactured material which started as a fixed-use product such as Chinese paper, was now having to meet competition from multi-use plastic as he anticipated what would later be termed 'substitutes'. Commenting on

Japan's emergence, he identified their problems, strengths, and differences.

Further advice to managers introduced the Italian Vilfredo Pareto's (1848-1923) activity theory of 20% - 80%, where 80% of the results were in 20% of the activities, while 20% of results were in 80% of the activities. Returning to a point he had made some time earlier, Drucker suggested that the non-performing public organisations should be 're-privatised', which became the Thatcher Government's 'Privatisation'. Drucker was credited by them for the idea as they noted that hardly a country in the world did not utilise it for some of their public ownership.

As a bystander Drucker extended Schumpeter's observation that government had proved capable of doing one thing, creating inflation. Drucker recorded the ideas as then being 'capable of doing two things with great effectiveness' as he returned to Schumpeter's inflation and added *'and wage war'*.

The next book to emerge was 'Drucker on Management' (1970), published by the British Institute of Management, which is a collection of essays by Drucker, published in their then house magazine 'Management Today' or by their members 1964-1970. Again there are direct messages to managers. An interesting anecdote is a reference to

Walter Leaf (1852-1927), who was the most successful chairman of The Westminster Bank from 1917 to 1926. For Drucker his book 'Banking' (1926) was the best book on banking of its day with its clear style, and the integration of banking with the entire economy. Drucker also noted that not only was Leaf an outstanding banker but he was also a world-leading Homeric authority. Leaf's excellence at his professional job and his outstanding extra-curricular activity was appealing to Drucker as it was the pattern of how his life's work developed by making more than one outstanding contribution.

In the same year, 'Technology, Management and Society' (1970) was published. It argues that technological innovation emerged as in effect did history, with the irrigation cities that began in Mesopotamia, and that it was not until the 18th-century's Industrial Revolution that the same scale of advancement took place. This later event caused the need to review how this new society was organised, with management needing to be developed by the likes of Taylor, and Fayol. He also returns to Rathenau, who was the only one of these management pioneers who argued that management 'was an "objective"'; i.e. culture-free discipline – and no-one listened to him. By now Japan has become a regular inclusion in his writings, as he displays an understanding by a Westerner that was not obvious elsewhere in general management writing.

Although his style is to set the context of many of his ideas in the past, as we have seen, such as when he links technology from the irrigation cities to the Industrial Revolution, they are a foundation for a modern message as he progressed his ideas, to describe the computer as 'managing the moron'. He warns that if the computer is not making our organisations simpler, then it is being abused.

Nineteen-seventy-one produced two books that were unique in Drucker's writing. It was not that they were both collections of earlier essays, but that the American-market edition and the British edition had nine common essays with four unique to the American edition ('Men, Ideas and Politics' 1971) and three to the British ('The New Markets and Other Essays' 1971). The selection was made to appeal to two different markets. In both books Kierkegaard and Keynes were introduced. The mechanics of American society was explained as how their constitutional system works, together with their philosophical attitudes to pluralism. An education in Japanese management was provided.

Looking back, for Drucker 'The Practice of Management' (1954) was a watershed in his career as a management writer. His next book was his pillar because it was meticulously catalogued. 'Practice', by comparison, provides excitement; this latest book had the gravitas that could be produced only by someone at the top of his game. It was 'Management: Tasks, Responsibilities, Practices' (1974)

When Lord Robens wrote in 'The Director' (1974) 'If I were allowed only one book on management to take with me on my desert island I would certainly take this one', he was representing the views of the other reviewers. He also added that it would provide hours of stimulating reading and be an excellent book for reference. He did not mention that there were eight-hundred and thirty-nine pages to select from.

As a snapshot of the contents of the book, it collected his previous ideas, made refinements as necessary and then presented them in a new stimulating manner. Case studies included international businesses. He worked from the top down, explained the needs, and described how to form an effective board, and that the structure must be determined by the business's needs, and not by some inappropriate structure thrust upon it. He defined the relationship between business and government, and set down how the managers should do their jobs. He defined their new challenge as making the *knowledge worker* productive. He underscored the ethics of responsibility — that motivation needed the spirit of performance. He stressed the essentials of good communication; that people can only perform, if they know what and why they are expected to contribute.

He coined the term '*People are our greatest asset*', warned that the human machine is badly designed, and that you cannot 'hire a hand as the man always comes with it'. Later he added a personal message that we must 'develop our strengths and eliminate our weaknesses'. On ideas on people at work he introduced Warren Gamaliel Bennis (1908-1970) and Abraham Harold Maslow (1908-1970), whose work he partly related to Dostoevsky's 'Grand Inquisitor'. He advised on the problems of different-sized businesses from the small at the one end of the scale to the multi-national corporations at the other end. He warned that as businesses moved up the size scale, they needed changes in the structure which required meticulous attention to detail as it was a fundamental change, not a natural evolutionary process.

On education he confirmed that the talk about the crisis in universities was real. However some places have seized on the opportunities. 'In Great Britain there is the Open University, which uses television to make education available to anyone who is willing to do the work' (*Ibid*: 340). The lesson was that every organisation needed innovation to convert problems into opportunities.

Of the current reoccurring topic of top executives' pay, he believed that the ratio between the blue collar worker and the top executive of 1:12 was about correct. The '*extremely rich*' were the few heirs of pre-tax days, or owners of small businesses.[12] Drucker concluded his text by defining the legitimacy of management and decided it was 'to make

---

[12] There is an ongoing debate that now in businesses, employed chairmen, and CEOs can join the "wealth class" through the accumulation of their salaries, bonuses, share options, and protective contracts.

human *strength* productive' and also 'that personal *strengths* make social benefits'. If one runs one's eye down his index it will give a measure of how much ground he has covered, and the span of his intellect. Although several abridged versions of the book have been produced, they may be a convenience but they lack the essential intellectual impact.

After completing the book Drucker told a meeting with British managers that after finishing the book '*one sits down and reflects a little*'. He reflected on how the development of management had occurred during his lifetime. He told them that as managers you must educate workers, because nobody else will do it for you. Also you must remember that management is a practice that we learn by experience, because only then can it be converted into a principle, and that we need continual feedback between the two. Although our jobs have changed, it is not possible to go back even if we wished. It is up to us to decide what we are, what we stand for, and what is expected of us.

He also gave a word of warning that in America the mistake was that young managers should dedicate their lives to the company. He advised them that what they ought to do was to work hard, and perform well, but also have a life outside the company. Otherwise, when the inevitable disappointments of the middle-years arrive, there is nothing to fall back on except drink, affairs, or psycho-analysts.

After completing (Drucker 1974) his 'magnum opus' Drucker never needed to write as comprehensive a book again, as he had set down the principles, and practices of management as he saw them at that time.

In his essential continuing work he introduces a fresh new idea, refines, extends, and adjusts his earlier work to reflect the changes in society, and continues on his mission to extend and reshape the ways we think about, and apply, management.

Drucker continued with 'The Unseen Revolution: How Pension Fund Socialism Came to America' (1976). It was also reissued under the title 'The Pension Fund Revolution'. This was another tutorial with the emphasis on politics, society, and economics. Tracked was the change in society, and how the state has taken over the responsibilities that used to be those of the family. The population did not see it as a reward but as a right in what has become the 'welfare society'. As part of the fundamental social change, what has happened in America since World War II was that there had been an explosion of occupational pension provisions. He forecast that by 1985 employee pension funds will own half of corporate America. He again anticipated correctly that despite the current push to lower retirement age, it would eventually push beyond sixty-five, and a mandatory retirement day may be abolished as people extend their working lives.

The consequence of the pension fund revolution was what had happened, and what Marx failed to achieve: that the workforce should own their means of production. Contrary to Marx's prediction it had come about without a violent revolution. Drucker concluded that so fundamental are the changes that it is presenting American politics with the first opportunity for a genuine alignment since the 1930s: the opportunity to produce its own distinct brand of 'socialism'.

The next book was uniquely distinctive, being 'People and Performance – The Best of Peter Drucker on Management' (1977). Its distinctions were that it was Drucker's only text book and that it was specifically written for students. The index gives a guide to its contents with inclusion of Adam Smith, Jean-Baptist Say (1767-1832), Robert Owen, and Marx from the eighteenth and nineteenth-century. Schumpeter, Rathenau, Taylor, and Fayol represent the early twentieth-century followed by the developers of personnel management, Hugo Munsterberg, Maslow and the previously-mentioned Mayo, and McGregor.

In what was proving to be a novelty period in his book output, another solo type one-off was produced. It was called 'Management Cases' (1978), which simply described the contents. The title belies the range of the contents that span North America, South America and Europe geographically, while the organising ranged from universities, hospitals, religious dioceses, local authorities, local schools, military bases to local national and international organisations, chemical, electrical and car industries, meat packing, coal mining, banking, life assurance, and research libraries. The fifty cases are a stimulating extensive wide cross-section of organisations. In so doing it sets an exacting standard for other authors who intend to follow, and as usual with Drucker's work, it produced useful unexpected stimuli for the manager.

His next work was a novelty, an autobiography entitled 'Adventures of a Bystander' (1979). It is a collection of essays that are not only about his family, and his upbringing, but also profile the interesting people that he had met in his life in Austria, Germany, England, and America. It is a fascinating collection of characters, and experiences that challenge the reader to choose their favourite. His profile of Sloan is the most important for managers while his narrative on those later to become famous — The Prophets: Richard Buckminster Fuller (1895-1983) and Marshall McLuhan (1911-1980) — is an example of Drucker's unique skill in reading people, and situations.

Although Drucker separates his books into different groups, some bridge across his topic range; his next book 'Managing in Turbulent Times' (1980), was a prime example, as it was about politics, society, and the economy, but it was also a management book, as it was telling the managers how the changing environment was affecting them. His stark warning on inflation was that in the previous ten years, western and Japanese countries had been announcing 'record profits' which were illusionary, as very few had made a profit at all. He reminded his audience that the foundation of profit had to be the cost of staying in business. On a pragmatic note he recorded the reality was that higher taxes on businesses increased the practice of 'moon-lighting', or the 'black economy' as a reaction.

Although Karl Emil Maximilian "Max" Weber (1864-1920) was noted in (Drucker 1979), it was a social reference. Now Drucker conceded that Weber's 'bureaucratic management' was a phenomenon worldwide, and part of the institutionalisation in every developed country. As Drucker's priority was to promote his market-driven free-economy businesses management, he had now had to admit that different forms were needed, for the risk-adverse public sector.

Of the manager's job, the demands and challenges in these turbulent times are providing exciting tests not only in business, but also in public non-profit organisations. This by-line on the non-profits, which will eventually be called The Third Sector, is highlighting where Drucker's last new contribution will eventually be.

In his next book he reverted to his basic pattern, and centred on economics with his 'Towards The Next Economics' (1981). It is a collection of papers written for the American quality market including the 'Harvard Business Review'. The core of the essays is a fresh or variant examination of his previous areas including 'A User's Guide to MbO', a further review of 'After Fixed Age Retirement Is Gone'.

A review of the pressures on the environment produced a rational appeal by Drucker for protection, but he called for sympathetic regard to the needs of the population of poor countries. He continued that one should remember that the impact of the brain-buzzing environmental damages we have caused in developed countries was the consequence of success. His remedy is for America to put its own house in order and begin to correct the pollution backlog, changing the current deteriorations.

He stated that it is nonsense to believe that industry can pay for the remedy out of its existing profit. It is not large enough. The cost will have to be met from taxation, or price increases on goods, which is in effect a tax.

For those who are uncertain of Drucker's range of exceptional intellect, the paper 'A View of Japan Through Japanese Art' will provide convincing evidence to remove their doubt.[13]

---

[13] See 'Adventures of the Brush (1979) which was an exhibition catalogue that first included this chapter.

## His own seventieth birthday present

Drucker's next book 'The Last Of All Possible Worlds' (1982), was another first, being one of his two novels. He described them as an indulgence compared with his other writing, and a present for his seventieth birthday. It centred on the world of the wealthy Austrian London-based ambassador Prince Sobieski. Although the book did not achieve high sales it deserved a better reception as it was important as a historical novel that recorded important social patterns.

Drucker returned to his messages for managers with his 'The Changing World of the Executive' (1982). It is another collection of forty of his articles, mostly from his Wall Street Journal writing. They are in five groups of executive agenda, business performance, non-profit institutions, people at work and the changing globe. Returning to a previous topic of executives' pay, he forecast that an inevitable backlash was developing because business was not communicating a sensible compensation structure. Within this context, truly exceptional people, the 'stars' who make a 'break-through', should be paid proportionately without limit. The medal winner who contributes beyond "the call of duty" should also have exceptional rewards.

Again to revert to a previous topic of unsustainable social wage benefit, he examined the much-ignored labour-income ratio, which related labour costs to each sales unit. He warned that while the bulk of American manufacturing had enjoyed substantial prosperity, an 'American disease' had developed in the steel and auto industry. The danger of their excessive labour incomes was threatening their survival with GM exampled; it paid 50% to 100% more than the American industrial average. As the American average was equivalent to their German and Japanese competitors, they barely had enough left to modernise their plant, and develop fuel-efficient cars. Of the labour unions, Drucker's position was that in a modern society they were a necessary counter-force related to management and the corporations. However they must be accommodated within pre-set limits.

Drucker's interest in The Third Sector was recorded in an essay on 'Managing the Non-Profit Institute'. Japan was covered as before. India joined his consideration as it moved from its spinning-wheel technology. The book concludes with a reassessment of ethics as he starts from his Protestant base to consider the casuistry idea of general interest, and the need to protect jobs, and moves on to Confucian ideals of rule of conduct, definition of relationships that need to be mutually beneficial. Later he will warn that different cultures, mainly influenced by their religions, will interpret the same words differently. An example is the word 'responsible', which will have different connotations in different parts of the world.

He concludes that the 'Ethics of Prudence' should prevail, where managers shun behaviour that they would not respect in others, and conduct themselves as the person who they would want to see in the mirror in the morning.

In 1984 Drucker's second, and last novel was published, 'The Temptation To Do Good'. The theme of the book is a relationship between the President of a rising American university who tried to aid an incompetent teacher. It was written against the background of the extensive work that Drucker had carried out not only as a lecturer, but also as a consultant to American universities. It deserved better than the limited success it achieved.

After his last novel, Drucker again reverted to his normal pattern of writing with 'Innovation and Entrepreneurship' (1985). The book is recognised as the first management book on innovation and entrepreneurship. He tells us that *'entrepreneurship is neither science nor an art. It is a practice'*; as with all practices such as engineering or medicine, knowledge is a means to an end. Consequently a book such as this should be backed by years of practice. Drucker goes on to explain that his empirical research began thirty years before in the mid-fifties with mature students at the Graduate Business School of New York University.

He continues that he had been discussing the subjects in his management books for decades against the background that other management writers have only become interested in the subject in the last few years. The extensive index indicates the wide range of the book, as he linked entrepreneurship and innovation, nationally and internationally, to various-sized commercial organisations, public services, non-profit organisations, and churches. His esteemed Schumpeter is included for his monumental book *Business Cycles* 1939, which popularised Nikolai Dmytrievich Kondratieff (Kondralyer) (1892-1938) and his long wave cycles. Drucker tells managers that entrepreneurship can and must be learned, and that all managers must be entrepreneurs. Again the book is dedicated *'To Doris The Innovator and Entrepreneur'*.

'Innovation and Entrepreneurship' was the start of a run of six books on the subject of management. The next was: 'The Frontiers of Management: Where Tomorrow's Decisions Are Being Shaped Today' 1986), which is a collection of thirty-seven essays which although they had been previously published; the original intention was that they would eventually be published, collectively. Included is an Interview and for the first time an Afterword. The pattern of the book is described in its sub-title. It ranges from advice on currency exposure, Japan, Germany and quality education, white-collar productivity, and rules for successful acquisitions. His essay on 'Overpaid Executives: The Greed Effect', written in 1983, has a 1986 note that records that Lido Iacocca, the chairman of Chrysler, paid himself a multi-million dollar bonus, as he cut the blue-collar worker's wage by 30%. Drucker continues that the Iacocca failed to convince the labour union that the benefit load on the wage rates needed to be cut. Prophetically, Drucker forecasts that if the American automobile market turned down for five years it was likely to destroy the company. Drucker then moves to his aim for management, which was that it needed to be a discipline, with an organised body of knowledge. He then states that it *'can be learned and perhaps even taught'*.[14] He is now concluding that management is a 'liberal art'.[15] Also there is an interesting change of mind as he had previously maintained that management could only be learned, and could not be taught. Now he was uncertain. What he is consistent about, is that entrepreneurship could, and must, be learned.

On Japan, he again displays his competence on the subject and he records that Edwards Deming taught the Japanese quality control and introduced 'quality cycles', while Joseph Juran taught them 'Kanban' 'just in time' inventory delivery. The Bulgarian Elias Canetti (1905-1994) is first introduced for his crowd theory, the psycho-dynamics of the mass. Drucker supports Canetti's theory of sixty years ago that the central psychological problem of the twentieth-century was not the individual, but the mass movement, which led to Hitler, Mussolini and

---

[14] This is a move from his initial position, which was that management could only be learned and could not be taught. Where Drucker is definite is that entrepreneurship can be learned. His emphasis to managers is "and must be learned".

[15] This is of particular interest to Drucker academics, who are devoting considerable thought to this statement.

Joseph Stalin (1879-1953)[16]. Again the essentials of Gestalt are again explained but not the evolving personalities.[17]

'Frontiers' has an outstanding example of one of the many ways that Drucker was unique. While many were acclaiming the Japanese for inventing 'Kaisen' continual improvement, Drucker was telling us that Thomas Watson Snr (1874-1956), the President of IBM, had invented it before them in the early 1930s.[18] In an interview he confirmed that he had come out of political journalism and his consulting work was now fifty-fifty, profit and non-profit. As another seventieth birthday present, he had become Professor of Japanese Art.

His published work continued with 'The New Realities' (1989), which marked his eightieth birthday. Keynes at opposites with Schumpeter, Keynes maintained that the velocity of money, the turnover of money was fixed. For Drucker, what we know is that Schumpeter proved in the mid-1930s that the velocity could change very quickly.[19]

---

[16] This is one of the very rare occasions where Drucker was behind events, as Canetti was relevant in (Drucker 1939).

[17] The Founders of modern twentieth-century Gestalt were the European psychologists Max Wertheimer, Kurt Koffa, and Wolfgang Kohler.

[18] See 'Quality Control Handbook' edited by JM Juran (1951) McGraw Hall, New York, Tokyo and London Chapter 9 Applications of Electronic Accounting Machines to Quality Control – IBM.

[19] Schumpeter credits the Paris-based Irish banker Richard Cantillon (1680-1734) with identifying the velocity of money in the mid-1750s. Cantillon also was the first to use 'entrepreneur' in a modern management form. Drucker did not reference Cantillon but was in good company as Schumpeter chided Adam Smith for not paying enough attention to previous economists.

He recorded that 'The Economist' derided his idea of privatising when he was the first to propose it in (Drucker 1969). Ten years later, British Prime Minister Margaret Thatcher had adopted it and a further ten years on, it was an international phenomenon.

## His last major venture at eighty-one-years of age

The publication of 'Managing The Non-Profit Organisation' (1990) marked the announcement of what was Drucker's last major venture. Rather than a new basic intellectual discovery it was a variation on his concluding discovery – management. Having first discovered management as business management in 1946, as his work progressed he had become aware that management in other organisations was different. There were the non-profits where the measure of achievement was the quality of service, and the provision of satisfaction, rather than the bottom line. The publication of the book coincided with the formation of the establishment of the American-based Peter F Drucker Foundation for Non-Profit Managers, which was founded by one of the contributors to (Drucker 1990), Robert Burford, and by Frances Hesselbein who had been the National Executive Director of the Girl Scouts of the United States of America, the world's largest women's organisation, before becoming the founding President of the Drucker Foundation.

Philip Kotler, the contemporary marketing guru, was another contributor and was credited for his repeatedly republished pioneering work 'Strategic Marketing for Non-Profit Institutions' (1971).

What Drucker highlighted was that half of America's adult population was a volunteer in the non-profit sector. They spent at least three hours a week in what is America's largest employment sector. This contribution was American society's most distinguishing feature. Drucker urged managers to look to this area for a fulfilling management career, or act as a volunteer to develop new skills, and widen their vision as managers.

In 1992 Drucker had two books published. The first, 'Managing for the Future', was a collection of thirty-nine essays that were written over a period of five years. They cover Drucker's range of interests aimed at their dimensions in the executive's world. As with his work pattern, he brings new insights to his previous ideas while also developing new ones. There are two interviews with Drucker in which he describes the reason for the book, and its purpose as sometime between 1965 and 1973 the old world changed, leaving behind the creed of the past. What had replaced it was not viable as government grew but became less effective. Innovation is exceeding anyone's imagination because a small gadget can now replace an established industry, causing labour employed to drop while output rises. It is to help executives perform in the again-changing environment that the book had been written.

The second book, 'The Ecological Vision: Reflections on the American Condition', comprises thirty chapters, which are a collection of articles or papers published elsewhere. The utility of the book is that it made important material available in his more accessible books. It is in part a primer for those who need to know how the American political system and society focus. Also included are some old favourites published in his previous books.

This book was followed by 'Post-Capitalist Society' (1993), a penetrating insight into how society has been transformed. Drucker reviews his position on his early support for Max Weber's ideas from the beginning of the 20$^{th}$ century, which capitalism sprang from 'Protestant Ethics'. He admits that now there is insufficient evidence to justify the conclusion.

'Post-Capitalist' was a companion to 'The Unseen Revolution' (1976), which established that pension fund ownership by the workers had changed America, the largest capitalist country, also into a 'socialist' country. Drucker in 'Post-Capitalist', explained that the reason that he termed America 'socialist' is by using Marx's definition of socialism, being the employees owning their means of production. Drucker continued *'that capitalism probably peaked by World War I as the likes of Morgan, Rockefeller, Carnegie, Ford, and Rathenau…, have not been matched by later as powerful successors'*.

The wealthy still existed but their power had been replaced through the management revolution by the 'hired hands' of the 'professional manager'. Marx's proletariat had become the knowledge worker. Knowledge work had now become the new capital. This had placed an obligation on the worker of having to learn to live. Drucker reminded us that he had anticipated these changes decades before, which he did. He also concluded that the preferred structure of organisations in 1954 of decentralisation was no longer the appropriate patterns for all organisations, especially those knowledge-based where the individual members possess their own speciality. He parallelled the CEO role as the conductor of a symphony orchestra, who knows what is needed, and calls upon the appropriate contribution of the participants.

Drucker (1976), together with Drucker (1993), are classics. The contents of Drucker (1976) also included analysis, and commentary on the Nation State becoming the Mega-State, and the Nanny State, which are simultaneously threatened by terrorism. The comment by Drucker on the size of the State is a situation that he comments on in his early work. His argument had been consistent that the State is too big.

In the new order, money had also changed as 'Money knows no fatherland'. Drucker moved on with his next book 'Managing in a Time of Great Change' (1995). It had a similar pattern to 'Managing for the Future' (1995) with twenty-five chapters, which despite their apparent diversity, all had a common denominator of *changes* that had already irreversibly happened.

The book is divided into four sections:

1. Management
2. Information-based organisations
3. The economy
4. Society

He tells managers in the 'Post Capitalist' society what their new challenges are: that data is not information, that China and the Pacific Rim are the strong economies, with Japan under question. Although he makes no prediction regarding the future, he notes that forecasting the future, based upon predictions that are obvious, is not difficult. What are far more important are the changes that no-one would have predicted. He looks back ten years to 1985 and concludes that no-one would have predicted that the European Economic Community would produce petty bickering, and would not provide explosive growth. Now it is weaker in the world economy than when the European countries were independent. At the other end of the spectrum, no one would have predicted China's explosive economic growth.

The fundamental changes that were occurring in the world were causing organisations to examine their management, and change to meet the new challenges. They had to re-engineer themselves, resulting in removing unnecessary management layers, which have been acting as redundant relays. These unnecessary layers hinder communications, as each excessive layer defuses the message. Having previously pronounced on re-engineering, he now reinforced his message that it must be done. Down-sizing he condemned as destructive of workers, and of the organization, with the loss of their tacit essential knowledge.

Drucker broke yet again with his regular pattern of books with his next publication 'Drucker on Asia: A dialogue between Peter Drucker and Isao Nakauchi' (1997), first published in Japan in 1995. The Preface of the book described it as an interchange of ideas between Drucker, and Isao Nakauchi. They are described as two old men. Nakauchi was the principal owner-officer of a leading retail company in Japan, and had held public office. They both look at the same questions from their differing positions. Drucker sets the economic scene in Japan, and records that it was sadly lacking in the real-growth high-tech industries of genetics, bio-technology, software, information technology and new finance.

The two correspondents discuss the challenges in China, the borderless world, the knowledge society, entrepreneurship and innovation. They conclude that to meet these challenges there would have to be major reinventions of the individual, business, society and government. The outcome is summarised for managers by Nakauchi's conclusions of:

> **'The duty of executives**
>
> Through our exchange of letters, Professor Drucker, you have given me and other Japanese executives profound advice, and through this identified the tasks that we must address to create the future. You have set us a difficult but appealing challenge. It is the duty of executives and the 'executives of tomorrow' to meet this challenge. After all, the problem is our own; we must create the future by ourselves.
>
> As an executive charged with this tremendous responsibility for the future, I pledge to you and our readers that I will work with many other executives to follow the instructions that I have received from you. I will strive to fulfil your expectations by continuing to contribute to the process of creating the future as I have up till now'. *March 27, 1995*'

For students of Drucker the two most significant sections are the following. The first sets his objections:

> 'My publisher in Japan, Diamond, recently published selected essays of mine, written over the last fifty years, under the title

*The Future Which Already Happened (The Ecological Vision, 1993).* For this book, I wrote a kind of intellectual autobiography which constitutes the last chapter of the book. In it, I record the beginning of my work more than sixty years ago which was concerned with the balance between change and continuity. It was this concern that, ten years later, led me to the study of management. For I see in management, as you know, the specific organ of society that has to maintain the dynamic equilibrium between change and continuity, without which societies, organizations and individuals perish'. (Page 101)

The second most significant section for students of Drucker is Chapter 6 'Reinventing the Individual'. He begins by summarising that the individual needs to reinvent him or herself, be aware of change, and recognise social mobility in a world that is predominately knowledge rather than skill.

He sets down his seven experiences, which start with a mini-biography of life in Hamburg, and Verdi's influence. He adds to his striving for perfection, and quotes *'the greatest sculptor of ancient Greece, Phidias'*. Phidias was commanded to create statutes for the Parthenon in Athens circa 440BC. When completed, the city refused to pay for the sculptures because Phidias had carved backs to the figures that no-one could see. Phidias's argument was that the gods could see them.[20] He

---

[20] The sculptures were initially destroyed by the early Christians in the fifth-century

then described his other experience of developing one's own method of study, which involved critically reviewing once a year what he had done well or badly, and then taking the necessary action. He advised making sure that it was the current job that was being performed not one's last. Drucker continues that after fifty years as an international consultant, he finds that the most frequent problem is the failed promotion caused by people doing their old job. He further advises that when making significant decisions one must write them down, and then record what one expected the outcome to have been within the set time-frame.

Drucker said that he had followed this method and what it has taught him was what he could not do, and what he should not try to do. Of the things he could do, it taught him what improvements needed to be made. This is Drucker's advice: *'Play to your strengths and eliminate your weaknesses'*.

The seventh experience is that one may be remembered for writing books, giving lectures, or being a consultant but these were not enough because *'One does not make a difference unless it is a difference in the lives of people'*. (*Ibid*: 98-110)

---

AD. The remains have now been housed in the Acropolis Museum, Athens.

The other issues covered in the book were the new challenges of China, and the reinvention of the individual, business, society, and government. The knowledge society, entrepreneurship and innovation, and the collapse of the Keynesian 'Welfare State' were all variations on his long on-going subjects.

The next book to arrive was 'Peter Drucker on the Profession of Management' (1998). The book began with a Preface 'The Future Has Already Happened', which took us back to (Drucker 1959) as he again used demographics. The book was a collection of thirteen Harvard Business Review articles, selected by Nan Stone. Drucker insisted that the collection must be able to answer the reader's question: Why this book now? The answer was that the selections dealt with important issues of the day. The credits confirmed that of HBR contributors, Drucker was the most productive with more than thirty entries since 1950, six of which had won McKinsey Awards. All of the articles were for the manager.

As with all of Drucker's books it contained sage advice. His advice on demographics was that they tell about twenty years ahead, not seventy-five which is too far into the future. He stated that he did not make predictions because the future had already happened. However he did make relevant observations as to the reasons why the developed countries are so few in numbers, which was because they were so expensive. That the mobile knowledge worker was proving difficult to manage was because people identified themselves with their knowledge, rather than their organisations. That retirement age would rise before 2010 because seventy-five-year-olds are healthy. Winning strategies would be about information without organisations, yet 90% is within. This would become the major challenge.

Earlier in this paper we identified that Taylor underwent a metamorphosis in Drucker's hands. The beginning of the evidence can be seen in the 'Profession of Management' followed by (1999), (2001), (2002), (2003), and (2006).

Drucker summarised that Taylor's impact had a greater long-term effect than Marx, as Marx is a figure of the past, whereas Taylor's influences are ongoing. Taylor taught us not only how to work, but how to make the illiterate productive, which lifted people and backward countries out of poverty. He also taught us how to learn not only simple jobs but also complex intellectual ones by showing how we can learn incrementally to build a complex whole.

For Drucker, Taylor had an impact on the outcome of World War II, as his work organisation methods enabled American industry to increase production at a rate that was totally inconceivable for the Germans.

For Drucker, Taylor was still relevant because his influences were being further brought forward where they were having greater impact by amalgamating them with what Drucker considered as another production landmark, Quality Management.

Where Drucker considers we need to move forward from Taylor's ideas of a hundred years ago is that we need to manage people differently as what we now know is that:

> 'One does not "*manage*" people.
>
> The task is to lead people.
>
> And the goal is to make productive the specific strengths and knowledge of each individual.'

Following Drucker's re-assessment of Taylor, in (1998) Sloan also began to undergo a similar treatment. Whereas Taylor's ideas had been re-assessed to give them a contemporary relevance, Sloan was moving backwards. For Drucker, although Sloan with other management pioneers attempted to find the one correct structure for the enterprise (which Sloan determined as control and command decentralization), Drucker's assessment was that times had moved on. He concluded that although teamwork was presently all the rage, what we know now is that there is no one correct way to manage a business (1999), (2001), (2002), and (2006). The book concluded with an interview of Drucker by T George Harris on the practical implications of 'Post Capitalist Society' (1993).

Again, another change occurred in the pattern of the now ninety-year-old Drucker's book output with 'The Drucker Foundation Self Assessment Tool Participant Workbook' (1999). The book was for his Third Sector commitment, The Peter F Drucker Foundation for Non Profit Management. Not only was it for his Foundation but it was a set of instructions that he calls a Participant Workbook, which were fifteen Worksheets that were arranged under five headings that were the framework of organisations' management plan. The headings were as relevant as for-profit organisations :

What Is Our Mission?

Who Is Our Customer?

What Does The Customer Value?

What Are Our Results?

What Is Our Plan?

The manual concludes with a Self Assessment Tool Customer Form. The Foreword was by Frances Hasselbein. In the Introduction we are informed that when Drucker was eighty-eight years old in 1997, 'Business Week' called him: 'The most endearing management thinker of our time'. On 'Forbes' magazine cover he was headlined as 'Still the Youngest Mind'.

## Drucker at ninety-years-of-age

'Management Challenges for the 21$^{st}$ Century' (1999) was an extrapolation of ideas that affect the manager that had appeared in his previous books.

Drucker recorded that the idea for the book was to take the best from his management books of the last fifty years as a 'Drucker Retrospect'. As he set about his task he realised that it was not about looking backwards but looking ahead. It was yet another Drucker book in which each reader would find different favourites. What Drucker examined was that many of the basic assumptions that we had been taught as managers are no longer tenable, as they had outlived their usefulness, and were becoming serious obstacles. Samples included that there is only one correct organisation; being the one that fits the task; that principles did not tell us what to do, only what not to do. Maslow was still relevant as there was no one correct way of managing people. What we had now learned was that we did not manage people, we led them to make each individual productive by enabling them to contribute their strengths, and knowledge; that research was not computer modelling, which was a substitute for the 'test of reliability'. What was required first was small-scale testing, 'Piloting'; managers needed to keep their network active to find out what was really going on, remembering that data is not information. Again we were reminded of the birth-rate crisis in the maturing economies; that the Japanese miracle was over. 'It is to be hoped that the new European Bank will be able to maintain the Euro stable as a regional currency. But it is too much to hope that the individual countries within the European Union will then subordinate their domestic polices to the stability of the Euro'. (*Ibid*: 68)

'The Essential Drucker' (2001) was again a change of pattern with a selection of his earlier work. Previously we had seen that although Drucker classified his books under management, economics, politics, society, autobiography and fiction, the point that has been made is that all had management messages. This conclusion was reinforced by Drucker's introduction: *'The Essential Drucker is a selection from sixty years of my work writing on management. It begins with my book* The Future of Industrial Man *(1942).* Yet this book was consistently listed under Economics, Politics and Society as is the 2001 book.

> *'The chapters are a selection and have been made by my long life friend Mr Uida, my Japanese translator and editor for thirty years from his fifty-seven chapters in 2000, three Japanese volumes of my work. It has met with great success in Japan and is being published in China, Korea, Taiwan, Argentina, Brazil, Mexico – obviously America and the UK. As a recommendation he has translated many of my books into Japanese. He is thoroughly familiar with my work – in fact he knows it better than I do'.*

This book was a good introduction to Drucker's management work and made an important contribution to understanding Drucker. It reminded us how far, at ninety years of age, he had travelled with his ideas as he challenged some of his earlier assumptions — not because they weren't relevant at their time but because their environment had changed so much. As ever, there were many messages for the manager as he reminded us that "empowerment" is similar to what he proposed fifty years ago, when he talked about bringing people into the plan. Another item from his range of advice was that traditional cost accounting measured only the cost of an operation. In contrast 'activity-based costing' primarily records the non-productive costs, such as correcting defects, delayed deliveries, and all of the cost of not doing so. It recorded the items that traditional cost accounting could not record, as often 'downtime' could be equal to the cost of doing. What activity-based costing did was not only give better cost control; it gave 'result' control.

He returned to McGregor's Theory 'X' and Theory 'Y', which Drucker reminded us was much the same as he had said in 1954. He recalled that he and McGregor asserted that there was one best way to manage people. Drucker continued that this assumption underlined practically every book or paper on the management of people. Drucker admitted that he and McGregor were 'dead wrong', as had been proved by Maslow in his book 'Eupsychian Management' (1962), which by his 'hierarchy of needs' showed that people had to be managed differently. Another formative work on management of people, and their motivation was Frederick Irvine Herzberg's (1923-2000) 'The Motivation of Work' (1959) which introduced the 'hygiene factor' to people's behaviour as 'money alone does not motivate performance'.[21]

Further on, Drucker included some longstanding advice that, if people continually failed to perform their job, then it needed to be re-examined as it was beyond the capabilities of anyone. He termed this type of job as a "widow-maker' – perhaps a job that was always too difficult, or may have become so, through change. Always a futurist, Drucker considered what we all should consider doing in the second half of our life. He re-introduced his ideas again: that for the first time the individual could expect to outlive their business organisations, even if they survived beyond what he considered was their equivalent to a biological life of an average of thirty years for a business. As we could not expect the same organisation that we were with at thirty-years-of-age still being in existence when we were sixty-years-of-age, then we needed to think beyond work. He continued that being in the same job for forty or fifty years was too much for most people. The consequences were that they 'retired on the job', lost all joy of work, were bored, resulting in being boring, and depressive to themselves,

---

[21] Although Drucker somewhat dramatically declares Maslow proved him wrong, he had been previously exploring on similar lines. Maslow's book title 'Eupsychian' was a word he invented meaning 'moving towards psychological health'. His publishers wanted him to change the title, which he refused. As for Herzberg when he was told that Drucker had already stated what his book conveyed (1950: 134), his response was that his book was based upon empirical research.

and all around them. Drucker quoted examples of how famous people had managed their lives. Pablo Casals (1876-1973), the famous Spanish cellist, continued in his career until he died. Max Planck (1858-1947) had a second career when he was forty; in fact he had two second careers, while Albert Einstein (1879-1955) retired at forty 'to become a famous man'. Drucker continued that manual workers became mentally and physically tired, before they retired. When they did, they were happy doing nothing or having a hobby such as fishing. Knowledge workers were more mentally active, and as with all other workers they might have a second career in the voluntary sector. They might run the career parallel to their normal job.[22]

Previously it was noted that Drucker's books, regardless as to how he classified them, all had management messages. His next book 'Managing in the Next Society' (2002) was a further example.

It was a collection of essays on society for managers. Its purpose was to try to anticipate the type of society that managers might expect ten years ahead. The book is divided into four sections:

Information society

Business opportunities

---

[22] "To manage oneself increasingly requires preparation for the second half of one's life." Since Drucker's death there has been resurgence in interest in his life, and work. As could be anticipated, his management ideas are receiving further examination. Less predictable is the considerable interest in Drucker's ideas of how one should live one's life.

The changing world economy

The next society

He compared E-commerce, and the related IT, with the impact that the arrival of the railways one-hundred and seventy years ago, which had also unexpectedly changed the economy, politics, and society.

Drucker creates a journey through each section as he describes how information was changing the ways we managed. As with so many of his books he ranges far and wide, old and new. Old favourites are included such as the Gutenberg press of 1455, which made the knowledge revolution possible, Luther's Bible, which enabled Protestantism, and Machiavelli's book 'The Prince' (1513), which described political tactics. Henry Ford is reclassified as an assembler rather than a manufacturer. Newer arrivals are Tom Watson Jnr, who is credited with making computer literacy possible. He is joined by Jack Welch, and Warren Buffett, for their respective contemporary contribution.

As direct messages for managers again, particularly for the CEO, is that it is results that count and not charisma, as he reviewed his own ideas on leadership at work, which go back to when Drucker was setting-down his ideas on management in Drucker (1954). What he makes clear is that leadership and management had to be considered separately for managers to understand what they could contribute.

Drucker starts his position with a reference to the Greek general Xenophon (431BC-354BC) and his book 'Cyropaedia', which (Drucker 1954) regarded as still the best work on leadership. What Drucker argues is that while there is no substitute for leadership, the supply of leaders is too unpredictable for management to rely on. His answer is to provide sufficient managers to lead by developing management as a discipline, so that it can be learned.

Part of the discipline would be that by the correct practices, development would be 'whatever potential for leadership there is in their management group'.

> 'They should also lay the foundation for the right kind of leadership. For leadership is not magnetic personality – that can just as well be demagoguery. It is not 'making friends and influencing people'[23] – that is salesmanship. Leadership is the lifting of a man's vision to higher sights, the raising of a man's performance to a higher standard, the building of a man's personality beyond its normal limitations. Nothing better

---

[23] 'Making Friends and Influencing People' (1937) is the title of Dale Carnegie's (originally Carnagey) (1888-1955) book. Carnegie does not find his way into any of Drucker's texts examined.

prepares the ground for such leadership than a spirit of management that confirms in the day-to-day practices of the organization strict principles of conduct and responsibility, high standards of performance, and respect for the individual and his work. For leadership, too, the words of the savings bank advertisement apply: "Wishing won't make it so; doing will'". (1954:157)

Drucker's summary of his ideas on leadership in management is that it is based upon the example of work, the practice of responsibility, and trust that had to be earned, and maintained.

Drucker continues that there are many challenges for management in their changing world, where the Internet would perhaps eventually become the major source for goods, as people had to learn that nothing changes faster than distribution channels. Even the mass-producing car manufacturers are making to order as Activity-Based Accounting progresses into the Economic Chain Activity. Drucker draws attention to the problems that all businesses have; not knowing about their non-customers. Although it is not an easy task to find out about them, it is still a problem even for the giants. If they have 30% of the market, there are still 70% who do not trade with them.

What Drucker was certain about was that fifteen years from then, governance of corporations would be different. Drucker gives an international round-up, and concludes in the developed world that pensions are under-funded. America is a self-help society with a large non-profit content, which provided many social services whereas in Europe the services were government provided. He is optimistic about American population balance as it was young in profile; America also has a conditioning to accept immigration. In contrast, Germany and Japan have structural problems of an aging population with resistance to immigration. For society the last century began with economic issues; this one has social issues.

'A Functioning Society' (2003) was another selection from previously published works, which concentrated on his interest in community, and society. Drucker explained that although he was best known for his management writing it had neither been his first nor foremost concern, as he became interested in it only through his work on community and society. The Introduction gave a profile of Drucker's early life up to his early years in America.

Of some of the topics covered, on the Mega-state, in 1918 Schumpeter warned that the fiscal state would eventually undermine governments' ability to govern. Fifteen years later Keynes hailed it as the great liberator, no longer limiting spending restraints, and that the fiscal state governments could govern efficiently. We now know that Schumpeter was correct.

The book was in the pattern of Drucker's life's work, being a continual educator for his audience. An example is his description of the often-confused definition of pluralism. He describes its original form of influence based upon power centres confined to geographic areas as dukes, counts, and even yeomen, who filled into a set order. Each centre was set in its area and was a total community, which accepted the existing organisation of social activity and political life. Now he identified that in the last half-century there is a *'new pluralism'*, while the old American pluralism still exists with the American federal system of defined areas for the federal government state, governments, and the municipalities controlling their allocated responsibilities, of the police, defence, justice, and tax powers. The new pluralists of special-purpose institutions were defined, not by geography but by function, such as hospitals, and universities; they were the new society of organisation.

By the year 2000, Drucker's health was deteriorating and his work became a personal battle. His long time colleague at Claremont, Professor Joseph Maciariello, devoted much of his time to helping Drucker organise his writing. In the year of Drucker's death, 2005, 'The Daily Drucker' was published. It is a page-a-day diary of three-hundred-and-sixty-six days of extracts from Drucker's work. It covers the range of Drucker's ideas. Its recommendation is that it is the book for students to start with, to determine if Drucker has any appeal for them.

Posthumously published is another joint venture with Maciariello 'The Effective Executive in Action' (2006). Drucker describes Maciariello as his colleague and friend of thirty years. He also credits him with ideas for the book, and for knowing his work better than Drucker.

It is an open format in a workshop form, where Drucker's ideas are presented with space for the reader to write their reactions and opinions. For this writer the most appealing message is a reflection of Drucker's old-world charm.

> 'Manners are the lubricating oil of an organization. It is a law of nature that two moving bodies in contact with each other create friction. This is as true for human beings as it is for inanimate objects. Manners – simple things, like saying "please" and "thank you" and knowing a person's name or asking after her family – enable two people to work together whether they like each other or not. Bright people, especially bright young people, often do not understand this. If analysis shows that someone's brilliant work fails again and again as soon as co-operation from others is required, it probably

indicates a lack of courtesy – that is, a lack of manners'. (2006: 75)

The next of the crop of posthumous books of Drucker's work to date is 'Classic Drucker: Essential Wisdom of Peter Drucker' from the pages of the 'Harvard Business Review' (HBR). The dust cover quotes 'Business Week' as calling him 'The Man Who Invented Management'. The editor credits Drucker for producing some of his best ideas for the HBR, which he did. It is easy to become blasé about Drucker as his ideas roll out to the extent that his student have come to expect. Often it was not his constructed argument that had the most impact, but his one-liners such as 'Corporations, once built to last like pyramids, are now more like tents'.

The last to date, but predictably with more to follow of the posthumous books of Drucker's work, is 'The Drucker Lectures' (2010) by R Wartzman, Executive Director of The Drucker Institute. It is another essential Drucker book. Although they have been written over sixty years, all of the lectures are relevant; some are timeless, and could have been written yesterday.

Important from a historical aspect is the *knowledge worker* and the *knowledge society* (1994), which is from the Edwin L Godkin lecture at Harvard University.

You'll find your own favourites to choose from, such as:

'Managing Oneself 1999

*In a few hundred years, when the history of our time will be written from a long-term perspective, I think it is very probable that the most important event these historians will see is not technology. It is not the Internet. It is not e-commerce. It is an unprecedented change in the human condition. For the first time, and I mean that literally, very substantial and rapidly growing numbers of people have choices. For the first time, they will have to manage themselves. And let me say, we are totally unprepared for it.*

*A good many of you were kind enough to send me questions in advance of this talk, and I am grateful. But not one of these 28 questions deals with managing oneself. They are all focused on "How do I relate to other people?" "How do other people relate to me?" "How do I make myself more appreciated?" Not one of them says, "What do I do with myself? And how do I find out?" And this is not surprising. Throughout history, practically nobody had any choice.*

*Up until 1900, even in the most highly developed countries, the overwhelming majority followed their father, if they were lucky. There was only downward mobility; there was no upward mobility. If your father was a peasant farmer, you were a peasant famer. If he was a craftsman, you were a craftsman. And so on. And now suddenly a very large minority of people – and it's growing – have choices.'*

As previously noted, the recommendation for starting with Drucker is 'The Daily Drucker'; now added are two other recommendations, as an appropriate introduction to Drucker — this Harvard tribute and Drucker's Lectures. Of the Harvard Tribute it is the first chapter, which has also been published separately, which can probably claim to be the smallest orthodox form of serious management book published. This pocket book is 'Managing Oneself' (2008). Why it is so important is that it challenges the reader to self-examine how they learn, and how they work, by asking the simple but profound questions: 'Do we learn by writing, talking, reading or listening'? What are my strengths'? 'How do I perform'? 'What are my values'? 'Where do I belong'?

As for Drucker's other book writing, what have been identified are Drucker's contributions, as editor, chapter writer, or contributor:

As the editor, where the contents followed the title of 'Preparing Tomorrow's Business Leaders Today' (1969); as a contributor to 'Power and Democracy in America' (1961); as the writer (of one of the five chapters) of 'Individual Freedom and Government In A Society of Super Powers'. This work was a historiographical travelogue of the evolution of politics since the beginning of the twentieth-century.

As a contributor to 'Technology in Western Civilizations Vol II', edited by Kranzberg and Pursel, London, New York; Oxford University Press. Two chapters from his 'Technology Management and Society' (1970) are reproduced as Chapter 4 – Technical Trends in the Twentieth Century and Chapter 5 – Technology and West Civilization. Drucker also contributed to 'Harvard Business Review on Management' (1975) where Drucker wrote 'New Templates for Today's Organisations', which was a personal reflection on the period's organisations.

Again as a contributor he wrote the Introduction to Mary Parker Follett's 'Prophet of Management' (1995), edited by Pauline Graham. Drucker wrote about the significance of Follett. He said that in 1941 when he became interested in management, he asked around regarding whom he should read. Follett only came to his notice when the Englishman, and nearest equivalent to Drucker, Lyndall Fownes Urwick (1891-1983) — who had called Drucker 'The Manager's Professor' — read a draft of a Drucker article in 1951 and told Drucker he sounded like Follett. For Drucker this was his introduction to her work. He then credited her significance in his script.

## Overview

Drucker is the most significant thinker ever on management, and its relationship to the wider environment, an idea which he developed. Only Rathenau before him had set management in the wider context that included ethics, society, economics, and the practice of management. Before his death, Drucker had featured in every recognised compendium of management thinkers in the English language, and had had six books written about him. Since his death resurgence in the interest in his ideas has occurred, as twice as many books have been written about him than when he was alive. They salute the man who changed the way that we think of management for ever, as they recall that he has been the most quoted, and is the most awarded, and has more books written about him than any other of his genre.

Although titled the 'Guru's Guru', he never accepted the title of 'guru', which he said was used because people could not spell 'charlatan'. More fittingly, he can be described as the 'Master of Management', a true polymath.

Currently Drucker Societies are being added around the world to join those in the Americas, Asia, and Europe, where a hub is being developed based upon the Drucker Society of Austria.

As for his widow Doris, she is still active in not only supporting her husband's work but has her own interests including her first business, which she started when approaching her eightieth year in 1997. It is a device she invented with a partner to help control speech volumes with a general application, and also for those who are hard of hearing. She said her inspiration came from sitting through her husband's speeches, and shouting from the back of the room whenever his voice dropped. She is also involved as a board member of several non-profit organisations in her home state of California. That she is a lady of high intelligence, resourceful, and with a highly developed sense of humour is apparent from her autobiography (2004).

Of Drucker's work there is plenty of choice from his ten million words, half of which are in book form — the other half being papers and articles. What you may find helpful from his many tributes is Alan Kantrow's 1980 paper which poses the question 'Why Read Peter Drucker?' Included in his answer is: "Because a manager can profit from the ideas and from the discipline of mind by which they are formulated. As Dr Johnson recognised, to understand the book it is not 'their individual blossoms but to grasp the trunk hard only and you will shake all of the branches.' In the work of Peter Drucker grasp hard the discipline of mind."

When I met Doris Drucker, and her daughters Cecily and Kathleen in Vienna in 2009 at the First Global Drucker Forum, (designed, prepared, and organised by Dr Richard Straub, and his wife Dr Ilse Straub) I asked her daughters why a comment reoccurred in the reports of interviewers who had visited their home in Claremont: many recorded that their house was more modest than they would have expected from so successful a man. They cheerfully replied that he gave his money away to good causes.

This brings us back to Schumpeter (Drucker / Nakauchi 1997). When in Drucker's presence his father, a long time friend of Schumpeter, asked Schumpeter what he wanted to be remembered for, Schumpeter replied:

> "'You know, Adolph, I have now reached the age where I know that being remembered for books and theories is not enough. One does not make a difference unless it is a difference in the lives of people". 'One reason my father had gone to see Schumpeter was that it was known that he was very sick and would not live long. Schumpeter died five days after we had visited him'.

Drucker records that

> 'I have never forgotten that conversation. I have learned from it three things. Firstly, one has to ask oneself what one wants to be remembered for. Secondly, that one should change as

119

one gets older. It should change both with one's own maturity and with the changes in the world. Finally, one thing worth being remembered for is the difference one makes in the lives of people'. (Page 110)

This summarised Drucker's achievement.

When asked how an organisation should become 'Druckerized', he said that was not the aim, and that we should look to ourselves and how we and our organisation can make more of the strengths that we all possess.

He defined 'The 5 Most Important Questions' as:

1. What is Our Mission?
2. Who are Our Customers?
3. What Does the Customer Value?
4. What are Our Results?
5. What is Our Plan?

(Drucker 1999 (i) revised edition)

Subsequently, as the Drucker Society California extends its reach, it is now advising high school students to look to Drucker's ideas to improve their own performance and use the five questions as a template for their school work.

(Drucker *et al* 2008)

## About the Author

Peter Starbuck was born in 1936 in Birmingham, England. He initially qualified as a quantity surveyor while doing National Service in the Royal Engineers when based in Hamelin, Germany (1959-July 1961), while Elvis Presley was completing his conscription in Berlin. The Berlin Wall was built a month later in the August.

It was during his time in Germany that he first became involved in his voluntary work, an interest he has continued with. Returning to civilian life he continued his career with an international construction contractor and further qualified in building management, and then general management.

In 1963 he moved to the rural West Midlands to manage a local building contractor and house builder. He has worked independently since 1966 when he commenced with partners his own construction training and house building business, which was sold in 1987. This was the first of his many ongoing entrepreneurial ventures.

It was during this period, at the end of 1974, that he became aware of the work of Peter Drucker when he read Drucker's *Magnum Opus* 'Management: Tasks, Responsibilities and Practices'. He was an immediate convert to Drucker's ideas, to which he could relate practically. Not only did he find Drucker's ideas applicable to business but also to the varied public and charitable organisations that he was involved with in education, health, social housing, training and the water industry.

What he discovered in all organisations — publics, private and the voluntary sector — was that if they applied Drucker's ideas they succeeded, while in contrast if they did not, then they at least struggled, or at worst failed. What he promised was that if he ever found the time he would study Drucker's books and identify the essential messages for young managers who never had the time to make the discoveries themselves — the object being that they would not repeat the mistakes of the past.

Twenty years ago in 1992 Peter Starbuck's work pattern changed from production to intellectual organisations and he was able to rearrange his work-load to devote half of his time to studying the works of Drucker and other related thinkers. Not anticipated was the result of his study being formalised in a doctorate on the Genesis of Drucker's Ideas. The consequence is that he is now accepted as an expert on the works of Drucker. From his private "think tank" he lectures and writes extensively on management-related issues.

He holds fellowships with the Royal Institute of Chartered Surveyors, the Chartered Institute of Building and the Chartered Management Institute and a Doctorate of Philosophy from the Open University Business School.

When people ask if he is related to 'Starbucks Coffee' he informs them that the only association is that the coffee chain adapted the name from one of his ancestors, the Quaker Edward Starbuck of Viking descent, who was born in Derbyshire, England, in 1604, and who became one of the original settlers in Nantucket, Cape Cod, USA, in 1659, and died there in 1690. He was also one of the founders of their whaling industry.

peterstarbuck@ic24.net

# BIBLIOGRAPHY

- Berle, A & Means, G (1933) *The Modern Corporation and Private Property*, New York: The McMillan Company
- Burnham, J (1941) *The Managerial Revolution*, Harmondsworth, England, New York: Penguin Books Ltd
- Carnegie, D (1913) *How To Win Friends and Influence People*,
- Chandler Jnr, A D (1962) *Strategy and Structure: Chapters in the History of the American Industrial Enterprise*, Massachusetts, London: The MIT Press
- Chaplin, C (1936) *Modern Times*, (Film) Hollywood United Artists
- Churchill W (1939), *Times Literary Supplement*, London; Times Newspapers
- Crowther.S (1926), *Patterson. John. H. Pioneer in Industrial Welfare*, New York Garden City Printing Company.
- De Tocqueville, F (1835 & 1840) *De La Démocratie en Amérique (Democracy in America)*, London: Oxford University Press
- Dostoevsky, F (1880) (1990 used) *The Grand Inquisitor*, New York: A Frederick Ungar Book Continuum
- Drucker, D (2004) *Invent Radium or I'll Pull Your Hair,* Chicago and London: The University Of Chicago Press
- Drucker, P F (1933) *Die Rechtfertigung des Volkerrechts aus dem Staatswillen (The Justification of International Law and the Will of the*

*State)*, Helf 8 Vienna: Walthar Schücking, Karl Strupp und Hans Wehburg

- Drucker, P F (1933) *Fr J Stahl; Konservative Staatslehre & Geschichtliche Entwicklung (Fr J Stahl; Conservative Theory of the State and Historical Development)*, Tübingen: J C B Mohr
- Drucker, P F (1936) *Die Judenfrage in Deutschland (The Jewish Question in Germany)*, Wein Austria: Gsur u Co
- Drucker, P F (1939) *The End of Economic Man*, London, Toronto: William Heinemann
- Drucker, P F (1942) *The Future of Industrial Man*, New York: The John Day Company
- Drucker, P F (1946) *Concept of the Corporation*, New York: The John Day Company
- Drucker, P F (Autumn 1946) *Keynes: Economics as a Magical System,* Charlottesville, Virginia: Virginia Quarterly Review
- Drucker, P F (Autumn 1949) *The Unfashionable Kierkegaard*, Tennessee: Sewanee Review, University of the South
- Drucker, P F (1950) *The New Society*, London: William Heinemann
- Drucker, P F (1954) *The Practice of Management*, London: Heron Books
- Drucker, P F (1955) *America's Next Twenty Years*
- Drucker, P F (1959) *Landmarks of Tomorrow*, New York: Harper Brothers

- Drucker, P F (1964) *Managing For Results*, New York: Harper & Row
- Drucker, P F (1966) *The Effective Executive*, New York, London: Harper & Row
- Drucker, P F (1969) *The Age of Discontinuity*, New York: Harper & Row
- Drucker, P F (1970) *Drucker on Management*
- Drucker, P F (1970) *Technology, Management & Society*, London: Heinemann
- Drucker, P F (1971) *Men, Ideas and Politics*, New York, London: Harper & Row
- Drucker, P F (1971) *The New Markets… and Other Essays*, London: Heinemann
- Drucker, P F (1974) *Management: Tasks, Responsibilities and Practices*, London: Heinemann
- Drucker, P F (1976) *The Unseen Revolution: How Pension Fund Socialism Came To America*, London: Heinemann
- Drucker, P F (1977) *People and Performance: The Best of Peter Drucker on Management*, London: Heinemann
- Drucker, P F (1978) *Management Cases*, London: Heinemann
- Drucker, P F (1979) *Adventures of a Bystander*, New York, London: Harper & Row
- Drucker, P F (1980) *Managing in Turbulent Times*, New York, London: Harper & Row

- Drucker, P F (1981) *Towards the Next Economics and other essays*, London: William Heinemann
- Drucker, P F (1982) *The Last of All Possible Worlds*, New York: Harper & Row
- Drucker, P F (1982) *The Changing World of the Executive*, London: Heinemann
- Drucker, P F (1983) *Modern Prophets: Schumpeter or Keynes*, New York City: Forbes Magazine, Forbes Inc
- Drucker, P F (1984) *The Temptation To Do Good*, London: Heinemann
- Drucker, P F (1985) *Innovation and Entrepreneurship*, London: William Heinemann
- Drucker, P F (1986) *The Frontiers of Management: Where tomorrow's decisions are being shaped today*, London: Heinemann
- Drucker, P F (1989) *The New Realities*, London: Heinemann Professional Publishing
- Drucker, P F (1990) *Managing the Non-Profit Organisation*, Oxford: Butterworth Heinemann
- Drucker, P F (1992) *Managing for the Future*, Oxford: Butterworth Heinemann
- Drucker, P F (1993) *Post-Capitalist Society*, London: Butterworth Heinemann
- Drucker, P F (1993) *The Ecological Vision*, New Brunswick, London: Transaction Publishing

- Drucker, P F (1995) *Managing in a Time of Great Change*, London: Butterworth Heinemann
- Drucker, P F (1997) *Drucker on Asia*, London: Butterworth Heinemann
- Drucker, P F (1998) *Peter Drucker on the Profession of Management*, Boston: Harvard Business School Publishing
- Drucker, P F (1999) *The Drucker Foundation Self-Assessment Tool Participant Workbook*, California: Jossey-Bass
- Drucker, P F (1999) *Management Challenges for the $21^{st}$ Century*, Oxford: Butterworth Heinemann
- Drucker, P F (2001) *The Essential Drucker*, Oxford: Butterworth Heinemann
- Drucker, P F (2002) *Managing in the Next Society*, Oxford, London, New York: Butterworth Heinemann
- Drucker, P F (2003) *A Functioning Society: Selections from Sixty-five Years of Writing on Community, Society and Polity*, New Brunswick, London: Transaction Publishers
- Drucker, P F (2006) *Classic Drucker*, Boston, Massachusetts, Harvard Business School Press
- Drucker, P F (2008) *Managing Oneself*, Boston, Massachusetts: Harvard Business School Press
- Drucker, P F *et al* (1969) *Preparing Tomorrow's Business Leaders Today*, New Jersey: Prentice Hall
- Drucker, P F *et al* (1975) *Review on Management*, Harvard Business Review

- Drucker, P F *et al* (2008) *The Five Most Important Questions You Will Ever Ask About Your Organization*, California: Jossey-Bass
- Drucker, P F & Maciariello, J A (2005) *The Daily Drucker*, Amsterdam, London, New York: Elservier Butterworth Heinemann
- Drucker, P F & Maciariello, J A (2006) *The Effective Executive in Action*
- Drucker, P F & Miller Dahl (1961) *Power & Democracy in America*, Westport: Greenward Press Publishers.
- Elon (2002) *The Pity of It All*, London: The Penguin Press
- Flaherty, J E (1999) *Peter Drucker, Shaping the Managerial Mind*, San Francisco: Jossey-Bass
- Germanicus (1937) *Germany The Last Four Years: An Independent Examination of the Result of National Socialism*, London: Eyre Spottiswood
- Given, W B (1949) *Bottom-Up Management*, New York: Harper & Brothers
- Graham, P (1995) ed. *Mary Parker Follett, Prophet of Management*, Boston, Massachusetts: Harvard Business School Press
- Huxley, A (1932) *Brave New World*, London: Chatto & Windus
- Juran, J (1991) (ed.) *Quality Control Handbook*, New York, Tokyo, London: McGraw-Hill
- Kantrow, A (1980) *Why Read Peter Drucker?,* Boston Massachusetts: Harvard Business Review, Harvard Business School

- Kaplan, R S & Norton, D D (1996) *The Balanced Scorecard*, Boston, Massachusetts: Harvard Business School Press
- Keynes, J M (1936) *The General Theory of Employment, Interest and Money*, London, McMillan
- Kierkegaard, S (1843) *Syrgt og Bievem (Fear and Trembling)*, London: Penguin Books
- Kotler, P (1971) *Strategic Marketing for Non Profit Institutions (sic Organisations)* New Jersey: Prentice Hall
- Leaf, Walter (1926) *Banking*, London: Williams and Norgate
- McGregor, D (1960) *The Human Side of Enterprise*, New York, Toronto, London: McGraw-Hill
- Machiavelli (1513) (1961 used) *The Prince*, London, New York: Penguin Books
- Maciariello, J A & Linkletter K E (2011) *Drucker's Lost Art of Management*, New York: McGraw Hill
- Marciano V M (1995) *Origins and Development of Human Resource Management*, London: British Academy of Management
- Maslow, A (1962) *Eupsychian Management*, Homewood Illinois: Irwin – The Dorsey Press
- Nelson, J (circa 2004/05) Bingley, Yorkshire: Emerald Group Publishing
- Polanyi (1944) *The Great Transformation*, USA: Rinehart & Company Inc
- Shlaes, A (2007) *The Forgotten Man*, New York: Harper Collins.

- Stein, G (2010) *Managing People and Organisations: Peter Drucker's Legacy*, UK: Emerald
- Wartzman R, (2010) *The Drucker Lectures*, New York: McGraw Hill
- Xenophon (circa 450 BC) *Cyropaedia (Life of Cyrus)*, London: The McMillan Company (1914), William Heinemann

# INDEX

# A
activity-based costing 104, 110
*Adventures of a Bystander* (Drucker) 80
Aquinas, Thomas 18, 71
*America's Next Twenty Years* (Drucker) 65
*Age of Discontiuity, The* (Drucker) 70

# B
Bakke, Edward Wright 53
balanced life (need for) 77, 106
*Balanced Scorecard* (Kaplan and Norton) 49
*Banker, The* 27
*Banking* (Leaf) 73
Barnard, Chester Irvine 51
Barzun, Jacques 46
Bennis, Warren Gamaliel 76
Berle, Adolf Augustus 44
Bibliography 125-132
*Big Business* – British title of *Concept of the Corporation* (Drucker) 47-52
*Bottom Up Management* (Given) 62
*Brave New World* (Huxley) 54
British Institute of Management 72
Brown, Frank Donaldson 48
Burke, Edmund 25

Burnham, James 44, 51

Burt, Sir Cyril Ludowic 61

# C

Calvin, Jean 18

Canetti, Elias 87

Cantillon, Richard 88

Carnegie, Andrew 45, 92

Carnegie, Dale 109

Casals, Pablo 106

Chandler, Alfred Du Pont Jnr 49

Changing world economy 107

Chaplin, Charlie 54

China 93-95, 98, 104

Churchill, Winston 41

computers (IT) 69, 99, 109-10

*Concept of the Corporation* (Drucker) 47-52

continual self-development 16

Cordiner, Ralph Jerron 57

*Changing World of the Executive, The* (Drucker) 83

create a customer and get paid 57

# D

De Tocqueville, Alexis 25

Dean, Joel 63

decentralisation 45, 49

Deming, William Edwards 66

*Democracy in America* (De Tocqueville) 25
demographics 65, 98-99
develop strengths and eliminate weaknesses 76
*Director, The* (Robens) 75
Dostoevsky, Fyodor Michaelovitch 18-21, 76
downsizing 94
Drucker, Adolf Bertram (father) 11, 23, 119
Drucker, Cecily (daughter) 119
Drucker, Doris (wife) 29-30, 34, 86, 119
*Drucker Foundation Self Assessment Tool Participant Workbook* 101
Drucker, Gerhard Augustin (brother) 11
Drucker, Karoline (mother, nee Bondi) 11
Drucker, Kathleen (daughter) 119
*Drucker Lectures, The* (Wartzman) 113
*Drucker on Asia* (Drucker) 94
*Drucker on Management* (Drucker) 72
Du Pont 49

# E

*Ecological Vision, The* (Drucker) 91
economics 35-40, 45, 53, 64, 93-94, 103
*Economist, The* 89
Einstein, Albert 106
*Effective Executive, The* (Drucker) 68-70
*End of Economic Man, The* (Drucker) 40-41
Equal opportunities 55
*Essential Drucker, The* (Drucker) 103

Ethics 15, 17-18, 26, 42, 45, 84

*Eupsychian Management* (Maslow) 105

European Economic Community (EU) 93, 103

executives' pay 76-77, 86-87

# F

Fayol, Henri Jules 61, 73, 79

*Fear and Trembling* (Kierkegaard) 18

Fisher, Irvine 41

five most important questions 120

Flaherty, John E 51

Follett, Mary Parker 116

Ford, Henry 41, 57, 92

Ford, non-contemporary manager 57

*Forgotten Man, The* (Shlaes) 41

*Fr J Stahl: Conservative Theory of the State and Historical Development* (Drucker) 24

*Frankfurter General Anzeiger* 22

Franz Ferdinand, Archduke 12

Freedom 21

Freud, Sigmund 12

*Frontiers of Management, The* (Drucker) 86

Fuller, Richard Buckminster 80

*Functioning Society, A* (Drucker) 110

*Future of Industrial Man, The* (Drucker) 42

# G

Gantt, Henry Laurence 61-62
    Gantt Charts (Bar Charts) 61-62
General Electric (GE) 46, 57
General Motors (GM) 47-51, 54, 84
    Brown, Frank Donaldson 48
    Mooney, James David 51
    Sloan, Alfred Pritchard jnr 48-50, 80, 100
*General Theory of Employment, Interest and Money* (Keynes) 28
*Germany: The Results of Four Years of National Socialism* (Germanicus) 27
Gestalt 16, 66
GI Bill of Rights 51
Gilbreth, Frank Bunker 61-62
Gilbreth, Lillian Evelyn Moller 61-62, 69
Given, William Barnes Jnr 62
Godkin, Edwin L 114
Graham, Pauline 116
*Grand Inquisitor, The* (Dostoevsky) 18-19, 76
*Great Transformation, The* (Polyani) 53
Gutenberg press 107

# H

Hamel, Gary 67
Herzberg, Frederick Irvine 105
Hitler, Adolf 17, 19, 34, 36-37, 42, 87
Hopf, Harry Arthur 61-62
human resources 60

Huxley, Aldous 54

# I

Iacocca, Lido 86

Industrial Revolution 73

*Innovation and Entrepreneurship* (Drucker) 86

*Invent Radium or I'll Pull Your Hair* (Doris Drucker) 30

# J

Japan(ese) 29, 66, 72, 74, 80-82, 84, 86-88, 93-96, 104, 110

Juran, Joseph Moses 66, 87

*Justification of International Law and the Will of the State, The* (Drucker) 23

# K

Kantrow, Alan 118

Kaplan, Robert 49

Katona, George 63

Keynes, John Maynard 28-29, 36-40, 53, 70, 74, 88, 98, 111

Kierkegaard, Soren Aabye 18, 70, 74

Knight, Frank Hyneman 53

knowledge worker 60, 71, 75, 92, 99

Koffa, Kurt 88

Kohler, Wolfgang 88

Kondratieff, Nikolai Dmytrievich 86

Kotler, Philip 90

Kuznets, Simon Smith 63, 71

# L

*Landmarks of Tomorrow* (Drucker) 65
Laski, Harold 32
*Last of All Possible Worlds, The* (Drucker) 83
leadership 108-110
Leaf, Walter 72-73
Lewis, John Llewellyn 51, 55
lifetime learning 71
Luther, Martin 18, 107

# M

Machiavelli 107
*Making Friends and Influencing People* (Carnegie) 109
Management by Objectives 34, 56-60, 82
management can be learned and perhaps even taught 87
*Management Cases* (Drucker) 79
*Management Challenges for the 21$^{st}$ Century* (Drucker) 102-3
*Management: Tasks, Responsibilities, Practices* (Drucker) 74
*Managerial Revolution, The* (Burnham) 44
managers not to leave unsustainable liabilities for their successors 54
*Managing for Results* (Drucker) 67-68
*Managing for the Future* (Drucker) 90
*Managing in a Time of Great Change* (Drucker) 93
*Managing in the Next Society* (Drucker) 107
*Managing in Turbulent Times* (Drucker) 80
*Managing Oneself* (Drucker) 115

managing people 100

*Managing the Non-Profit Institute* (Drucker) 84

*Managing the Non-Profit Organisation* (Drucker) 89

manners 113

Marciano, VM 60

Marx, Karl Heinrich 17, 21, 35, 41, 70, 79, 92, 99

Maslow, Abraham Harold 76, 79, 105

Mayo, Elton George 53, 79

McCormick, Cyrus Hall 61

McGregor, Douglas Murray 60, 79, 105

   Theory X, Theory Y 60, 105

McLuhan, Marshall 80

McNair, Malcolm Perrine 63

Means, Gardiner Colt 44

Mega-state, The 92, 111

*Men, Ideas and Politics* (Drucker) 74

Mistakes (learning from them) 63

*Modern Corporation and Private Property, The* (Berle and Means) 44

*Modern Times* (Chaplin) 54

Mooney, James David 51

Morgan, J Pierpoint 45, 92

*Motivation of Work, The* (Herzberg) 105

Munsterberg, Hugo 61, 79

Murray, Philip 55

Mussolini, Benito 17, 87

# N

Nakauchi, Isao 94, 119

Nelson, James 20-21

*New Markets and Other Essays, The* (Drucker) 74

*New Realities, The* (Drucker) 88

*New Society, The* (Drucker) 52

non-profit management 84, 89-90, 101

Norton, David 49

# O

Open University, The 76

overpaid executives 86-87

Owen, Robert 41, 79

# P

Pareto, Vilfredo 72

Patterson, John Henry 43

pension funds 78-79

*People and Performance* (Drucker) 79

people – our greatest asset 75

PERT Analysis 62

Peters, Thomas J 67

*Peter Drucker on the Profession of Management* (Drucker) 98-99

Phidias of Athens 96-97

Planck, Max 106

Polyani, Karl 53

*Post-Capitalist Society* (Drucker) 91

*Practice of Management, The* (Drucker) 56-63, 74

Prahalad, CK 67

*Prince, The* (Machiavelli) 107

Princip, Gavrilo 12

Procter and Gamble 54

purpose for living 17, 35

# R

Rathenau, Walther 41-44, 73, 117

re-engineering 94

Reiss, Elsa 14

Reiss, Sophy 14

Return on Investment (ROI) 49

Robbins, Lionel 32

Robens, Lord 75

Robinson, Joan Violet 32

Rockefeller, John D 45-46, 92

# S

Say, Jean-Baptist 79

Schmitz, Fritz 30

Schumpeter, Joseph Aloisius Julius 28-29, 37-40, 45, 53, 62, 68, 71-72, 79, 86, 88, 111, 119.

Schwarzwald, Dr Eugenia 14

Sears 57

Shakespeare, William 10

Shlaes, Amity 41

Sloan, Alfred Pritchard jnr 48-49, 80, 100

Smiddy, Harold Francis 57

Smith, Adam 35, 41, 51, 79, 88

Sobieski, Prince 83

Socrates 71

Span of Control 59

Spates, Thomas Gardiner 60

Stalin, Joseph 88

Stahl, Fr J 24-25

*Strategy and Structure* (Chandler) 49

Straub, Ilse 119

Straub, Richard 119

# T

Taylor, Frederick Winslow 46, 61, 79, 99-100

Teachers cannot spot entrepreneurs 55-56

Tead, Ordway 51

*Technology, Management and Society* (Drucker) 73

*Temptation to Do Good, The* (Drucker) 85

Tennessee Valley Authority Scheme 52

*Times Literary Supplement* 41

*Towards the Next Economics* (Drucker) 81

# U

Unions, Labour 50-54, 84
　　Lewis, John Llewellyn 51, 55
　　Murray, Philip 55
*The Unseen Revolution* (Drucker) 78-79, 91
Urwick, Lyndall Fownes 116

# V

Verdi, Giuseppe Fortunio Francesco 16, 96
*Virginia Quarterly Review* 29
volunteers 90
von Bohm-Bawerk, Eugen 52

# W

Wartzman, Rick 113
Waterman, Robert N Jnr 67
Watson, Thomas jnr 108
Watson, Thomas snr 43, 88
Watt, James 46
Weber, Max 18, 81, 91
Wertheimer, Max 88
*Why Read Peter Drucker?* (Kantrow) 118
Workable society 21, 25, 35

# X

Xenophon 108

# Y

Young, Owen D 46

# Z

Zola, Emile 71

# **NOTES**